C-4576   CAREER EXAMINATION SERIES

*This is your
PASSBOOK for...*

CUNY Office Assistant

*Test Preparation Study Guide
Questions & Answers*

COPYRIGHT NOTICE

This book is SOLELY intended for, is sold ONLY to, and its use is RESTRICTED to individual, bona fide applicants or candidates who qualify by virtue of having seriously filed applications for appropriate license, certificate, professional and/or promotional advancement, higher school matriculation, scholarship, or other legitimate requirements of education and/or governmental authorities.

This book is NOT intended for use, class instruction, tutoring, training, duplication, copying, reprinting, excerption, or adaptation, etc., by:

1) Other publishers
2) Proprietors and/or Instructors of "Coaching" and/or Preparatory Courses
3) Personnel and/or Training Divisions of commercial, industrial, and governmental organizations
4) Schools, colleges, or universities and/or their departments and staffs, including teachers and other personnel
5) Testing Agencies or Bureaus
6) Study groups which seek by the purchase of a single volume to copy and/or duplicate and/or adapt this material for use by the group as a whole without having purchased individual volumes for each of the members of the group
7) Et al.

Such persons would be in violation of appropriate Federal and State statutes.

PROVISION OF LICENSING AGREEMENTS – Recognized educational, commercial, industrial, and governmental institutions and organizations, and others legitimately engaged in educational pursuits, including training, testing, and measurement activities, may address request for a licensing agreement to the copyright owners, who will determine whether, and under what conditions, including fees and charges, the materials in this book may be used them. In other words, a licensing facility exists for the legitimate use of the material in this book on other than an individual basis. However, it is asseverated and affirmed here that the material in this book CANNOT be used without the receipt of the express permission of such a licensing agreement from the Publishers. Inquiries re licensing should be addressed to the company, attention rights and permissions department.

All rights reserved, including the right of reproduction in whole or in part, in any form or by any means, electronic or mechanical, including photocopying, recording, or by any information storage and retrieval system, without permission in writing from the Publisher.

Copyright © 2024 by
National Learning Corporation

212 Michael Drive, Syosset, NY 11791
(516) 921-8888 • www.passbooks.com
E-mail: info@passbooks.com

PUBLISHED IN THE UNITED STATES OF AMERICA

PASSBOOK® SERIES

THE *PASSBOOK® SERIES* has been created to prepare applicants and candidates for the ultimate academic battlefield – the examination room.

At some time in our lives, each and every one of us may be required to take an examination – for validation, matriculation, admission, qualification, registration, certification, or licensure.

Based on the assumption that every applicant or candidate has met the basic formal educational standards, has taken the required number of courses, and read the necessary texts, the *PASSBOOK® SERIES* furnishes the one special preparation which may assure passing with confidence, instead of failing with insecurity. Examination questions – together with answers – are furnished as the basic vehicle for study so that the mysteries of the examination and its compounding difficulties may be eliminated or diminished by a sure method.

This book is meant to help you pass your examination provided that you qualify and are serious in your objective.

The entire field is reviewed through the huge store of content information which is succinctly presented through a provocative and challenging approach – the question-and-answer method.

A climate of success is established by furnishing the correct answers at the end of each test.

You soon learn to recognize types of questions, forms of questions, and patterns of questioning. You may even begin to anticipate expected outcomes.

You perceive that many questions are repeated or adapted so that you can gain acute insights, which may enable you to score many sure points.

You learn how to confront new questions, or types of questions, and to attack them confidently and work out the correct answers.

You note objectives and emphases, and recognize pitfalls and dangers, so that you may make positive educational adjustments.

Moreover, you are kept fully informed in relation to new concepts, methods, practices, and directions in the field.

You discover that you are actually taking the examination all the time: you are preparing for the examination by "taking" an examination, not by reading extraneous and/or supererogatory textbooks.

In short, this PASSBOOK®, used directedly, should be an important factor in helping you to pass your test.

CUNY OFFICE ASSISTANT

DUTIES
CUNY Office Assistants perform clerical and daily office operations within various University academic and administrative departments. All CUNY Office Assistants perform related work.

SCOPE OF THE EXAMINATION
The multiple-choice test is designed to assess the extent to which candidates have certain abilities determined to be important to the performance of the tasks of a CUNY Office Assistant. Task areas to be tested are: clerical duties; records management; word processing/data entry; and communication responsibilities. The test may include questions which require the use of any of the following abilities:

1. **Deductive Reasoning**: The ability to apply general rules to specific problems to come up with logical answers. It involves deciding if an answer makes sense. It is also defined as Alphabetical and Numerical Coding, or the ability to classify or code files, records, correspondence, and forms according to their contents using a standard/prescribed classification system. Example: A CUNY Office Assistant would use this ability when determining which unit should receive a correspondence received from the public.

2. **Information Ordering**: The ability to follow correctly a rule or set of rules or actions in a certain order. The rule or set of rules used must be given. The things or actions to be put in order can include numbers, letters, words, pictures, procedures, sentences and mathematical or logical operations. Example: A CUNY Office Assistant would use this ability when filing items in alphabetical order in filing cabinets.

3. **Number Facility**: The degree to which adding, subtracting, multiplying and dividing can be done quickly and correctly. This can be steps in other operations like finding percentages. Example: A CUNY Office Assistant would use this ability when calculating the total amount of a student's bill.

4. **Matching**: The degree to which one can compare letters, numbers, objects, pictures or patterns accurately. It includes the ability to detect errors, make the appropriate corrections, and recognize similarities in clerical materials. Example: A CUNY Office Assistant would use this ability when comparing information in a student's application to the information entered in the computer system.

5. **Written Expression**: The ability to use English words or sentences in writing so that others will understand. Example: A CUNY Office Assistant would use this ability when writing an email.

HOW TO TAKE A TEST

I. YOU MUST PASS AN EXAMINATION

A. WHAT EVERY CANDIDATE SHOULD KNOW

Examination applicants often ask us for help in preparing for the written test. What can I study in advance? What kinds of questions will be asked? How will the test be given? How will the papers be graded?

As an applicant for a civil service examination, you may be wondering about some of these things. Our purpose here is to suggest effective methods of advance study and to describe civil service examinations.

Your chances for success on this examination can be increased if you know how to prepare. Those "pre-examination jitters" can be reduced if you know what to expect. You can even experience an adventure in good citizenship if you know why civil service exams are given.

B. WHY ARE CIVIL SERVICE EXAMINATIONS GIVEN?

Civil service examinations are important to you in two ways. As a citizen, you want public jobs filled by employees who know how to do their work. As a job seeker, you want a fair chance to compete for that job on an equal footing with other candidates. The best-known means of accomplishing this two-fold goal is the competitive examination.

Exams are widely publicized throughout the nation. They may be administered for jobs in federal, state, city, municipal, town or village governments or agencies.

Any citizen may apply, with some limitations, such as the age or residence of applicants. Your experience and education may be reviewed to see whether you meet the requirements for the particular examination. When these requirements exist, they are reasonable and applied consistently to all applicants. Thus, a competitive examination may cause you some uneasiness now, but it is your privilege and safeguard.

C. HOW ARE CIVIL SERVICE EXAMS DEVELOPED?

Examinations are carefully written by trained technicians who are specialists in the field known as "psychological measurement," in consultation with recognized authorities in the field of work that the test will cover. These experts recommend the subject matter areas or skills to be tested; only those knowledges or skills important to your success on the job are included. The most reliable books and source materials available are used as references. Together, the experts and technicians judge the difficulty level of the questions.

Test technicians know how to phrase questions so that the problem is clearly stated. Their ethics do not permit "trick" or "catch" questions. Questions may have been tried out on sample groups, or subjected to statistical analysis, to determine their usefulness.

Written tests are often used in combination with performance tests, ratings of training and experience, and oral interviews. All of these measures combine to form the best-known means of finding the right person for the right job.

II. HOW TO PASS THE WRITTEN TEST

A. NATURE OF THE EXAMINATION

To prepare intelligently for civil service examinations, you should know how they differ from school examinations you have taken. In school you were assigned certain definite pages to read or subjects to cover. The examination questions were quite detailed and usually emphasized memory. Civil service exams, on the other hand, try to discover your present ability to perform the duties of a position, plus your potentiality to learn these duties. In other words, a civil service exam attempts to predict how successful you will be. Questions cover such a broad area that they cannot be as minute and detailed as school exam questions.

In the public service similar kinds of work, or positions, are grouped together in one "class." This process is known as *position-classification*. All the positions in a class are paid according to the salary range for that class. One class title covers all of these positions, and they are all tested by the same examination.

B. FOUR BASIC STEPS

1) Study the announcement

How, then, can you know what subjects to study? Our best answer is: "Learn as much as possible about the class of positions for which you've applied." The exam will test the knowledge, skills and abilities needed to do the work.

Your most valuable source of information about the position you want is the official exam announcement. This announcement lists the training and experience qualifications. Check these standards and apply only if you come reasonably close to meeting them.

The brief description of the position in the examination announcement offers some clues to the subjects which will be tested. Think about the job itself. Review the duties in your mind. Can you perform them, or are there some in which you are rusty? Fill in the blank spots in your preparation.

Many jurisdictions preview the written test in the exam announcement by including a section called "Knowledge and Abilities Required," "Scope of the Examination," or some similar heading. Here you will find out specifically what fields will be tested.

2) Review your own background

Once you learn in general what the position is all about, and what you need to know to do the work, ask yourself which subjects you already know fairly well and which need improvement. You may wonder whether to concentrate on improving your strong areas or on building some background in your fields of weakness. When the announcement has specified "some knowledge" or "considerable knowledge," or has used adjectives like "beginning principles of…" or "advanced … methods," you can get a clue as to the number and difficulty of questions to be asked in any given field. More questions, and hence broader coverage, would be included for those subjects which are more important in the work. Now weigh your strengths and weaknesses against the job requirements and prepare accordingly.

3) Determine the level of the position

Another way to tell how intensively you should prepare is to understand the level of the job for which you are applying. Is it the entering level? In other words, is this the position in which beginners in a field of work are hired? Or is it an intermediate or advanced level? Sometimes this is indicated by such words as "Junior" or "Senior" in the class title. Other jurisdictions use Roman numerals to designate the level – Clerk I, Clerk II, for example. The word "Supervisor" sometimes appears in the title. If the level is not indicated by the title, check the description of duties. Will you be working under very close supervision, or will you have responsibility for independent decisions in this work?

4) Choose appropriate study materials

Now that you know the subjects to be examined and the relative amount of each subject to be covered, you can choose suitable study materials. For beginning level jobs, or even advanced ones, if you have a pronounced weakness in some aspect of your training, read a modern, standard textbook in that field. Be sure it is up to date and has general coverage. Such books are normally available at your library, and the librarian will be glad to help you locate one. For entry-level positions, questions of appropriate difficulty are chosen – neither highly advanced questions, nor those too simple. Such questions require careful thought but not advanced training.

If the position for which you are applying is technical or advanced, you will read more advanced, specialized material. If you are already familiar with the basic principles of your field, elementary textbooks would waste your time. Concentrate on advanced textbooks and technical periodicals. Think through the concepts and review difficult problems in your field.

These are all general sources. You can get more ideas on your own initiative, following these leads. For example, training manuals and publications of the government agency which employs workers in your field can be useful, particularly for technical and professional positions. A letter or visit to the government department involved may result in more specific study suggestions, and certainly will provide you with a more definite idea of the exact nature of the position you are seeking.

III. KINDS OF TESTS

Tests are used for purposes other than measuring knowledge and ability to perform specified duties. For some positions, it is equally important to test ability to make adjustments to new situations or to profit from training. In others, basic mental abilities not dependent on information are essential. Questions which test these things may not appear as pertinent to the duties of the position as those which test for knowledge and information. Yet they are often highly important parts of a fair examination. For very general questions, it is almost impossible to help you direct your study efforts. What we can do is to point out some of the more common of these general abilities needed in public service positions and describe some typical questions.

1) General information

Broad, general information has been found useful for predicting job success in some kinds of work. This is tested in a variety of ways, from vocabulary lists to questions about current events. Basic background in some field of work, such as sociology or economics, may be sampled in a group of questions. Often these are principles which have become familiar to most persons through exposure rather than through formal training. It is difficult to advise you how to study for these questions; being alert to the world around you is our best suggestion.

2) Verbal ability

An example of an ability needed in many positions is verbal or language ability. Verbal ability is, in brief, the ability to use and understand words. Vocabulary and grammar tests are typical measures of this ability. Reading comprehension or paragraph interpretation questions are common in many kinds of civil service tests. You are given a paragraph of written material and asked to find its central meaning.

3) Numerical ability

Number skills can be tested by the familiar arithmetic problem, by checking paired lists of numbers to see which are alike and which are different, or by interpreting charts and graphs. In the latter test, a graph may be printed in the test booklet which you are asked to use as the basis for answering questions.

4) Observation

A popular test for law-enforcement positions is the observation test. A picture is shown to you for several minutes, then taken away. Questions about the picture test your ability to observe both details and larger elements.

5) Following directions

In many positions in the public service, the employee must be able to carry out written instructions dependably and accurately. You may be given a chart with several columns, each column listing a variety of information. The questions require you to carry out directions involving the information given in the chart.

6) Skills and aptitudes

Performance tests effectively measure some manual skills and aptitudes. When the skill is one in which you are trained, such as typing or shorthand, you can practice. These tests are often very much like those given in business school or high school courses. For many of the other skills and aptitudes, however, no short-time preparation can be made. Skills and abilities natural to you or that you have developed throughout your lifetime are being tested.

Many of the general questions just described provide all the data needed to answer the questions and ask you to use your reasoning ability to find the answers. Your best preparation for these tests, as well as for tests of facts and ideas, is to be at your physical and mental best. You, no doubt, have your own methods of getting into an exam-taking mood and keeping "in shape." The next section lists some ideas on this subject.

IV. KINDS OF QUESTIONS

Only rarely is the "essay" question, which you answer in narrative form, used in civil service tests. Civil service tests are usually of the short-answer type. Full instructions for answering these questions will be given to you at the examination. But in case this is your first experience with short-answer questions and separate answer sheets, here is what you need to know:

1) Multiple-choice Questions

Most popular of the short-answer questions is the "multiple choice" or "best answer" question. It can be used, for example, to test for factual knowledge, ability to solve problems or judgment in meeting situations found at work.

A multiple-choice question is normally one of three types—
- It can begin with an incomplete statement followed by several possible endings. You are to find the one ending which *best* completes the statement, although some of the others may not be entirely wrong.
- It can also be a complete statement in the form of a question which is answered by choosing one of the statements listed.

- It can be in the form of a problem – again you select the best answer.

Here is an example of a multiple-choice question with a discussion which should give you some clues as to the method for choosing the right answer:

When an employee has a complaint about his assignment, the action which will *best* help him overcome his difficulty is to
   A. discuss his difficulty with his coworkers
   B. take the problem to the head of the organization
   C. take the problem to the person who gave him the assignment
   D. say nothing to anyone about his complaint

In answering this question, you should study each of the choices to find which is best. Consider choice "A" – Certainly an employee may discuss his complaint with fellow employees, but no change or improvement can result, and the complaint remains unresolved. Choice "B" is a poor choice since the head of the organization probably does not know what assignment you have been given, and taking your problem to him is known as "going over the head" of the supervisor. The supervisor, or person who made the assignment, is the person who can clarify it or correct any injustice. Choice "C" is, therefore, correct. To say nothing, as in choice "D," is unwise. Supervisors have and interest in knowing the problems employees are facing, and the employee is seeking a solution to his problem.

2) True/False Questions

The "true/false" or "right/wrong" form of question is sometimes used. Here a complete statement is given. Your job is to decide whether the statement is right or wrong.

SAMPLE: A roaming cell-phone call to a nearby city costs less than a non-roaming call to a distant city.

This statement is wrong, or false, since roaming calls are more expensive.

This is not a complete list of all possible question forms, although most of the others are variations of these common types. You will always get complete directions for answering questions. Be sure you understand *how* to mark your answers – ask questions until you do.

V. RECORDING YOUR ANSWERS

Computer terminals are used more and more today for many different kinds of exams.

For an examination with very few applicants, you may be told to record your answers in the test booklet itself. Separate answer sheets are much more common. If this separate answer sheet is to be scored by machine – and this is often the case – it is highly important that you mark your answers correctly in order to get credit.

An electronic scoring machine is often used in civil service offices because of the speed with which papers can be scored. Machine-scored answer sheets must be marked with a pencil, which will be given to you. This pencil has a high graphite content which responds to the electronic scoring machine. As a matter of fact, stray dots may register as answers, so do not let your pencil rest on the answer sheet while you are pondering the correct answer. Also, if your pencil lead breaks or is otherwise defective, ask for another.

Since the answer sheet will be dropped in a slot in the scoring machine, be careful not to bend the corners or get the paper crumpled.

The answer sheet normally has five vertical columns of numbers, with 30 numbers to a column. These numbers correspond to the question numbers in your test booklet. After each number, going across the page are four or five pairs of dotted lines. These short dotted lines have small letters or numbers above them. The first two pairs may also have a "T" or "F" above the letters. This indicates that the first two pairs only are to be used if the questions are of the true-false type. If the questions are multiple choice, disregard the "T" and "F" and pay attention only to the small letters or numbers.

Answer your questions in the manner of the sample that follows:

32. The largest city in the United States is
    A. Washington, D.C.
    B. New York City
    C. Chicago
    D. Detroit
    E. San Francisco

1) Choose the answer you think is best. (New York City is the largest, so "B" is correct.)
2) Find the row of dotted lines numbered the same as the question you are answering. (Find row number 32)
3) Find the pair of dotted lines corresponding to the answer. (Find the pair of lines under the mark "B.")
4) Make a solid black mark between the dotted lines.

VI. BEFORE THE TEST

Common sense will help you find procedures to follow to get ready for an examination. Too many of us, however, overlook these sensible measures. Indeed, nervousness and fatigue have been found to be the most serious reasons why applicants fail to do their best on civil service tests. Here is a list of reminders:

- Begin your preparation early – Don't wait until the last minute to go scurrying around for books and materials or to find out what the position is all about.
- Prepare continuously – An hour a night for a week is better than an all-night cram session. This has been definitely established. What is more, a night a week for a month will return better dividends than crowding your study into a shorter period of time.
- Locate the place of the exam – You have been sent a notice telling you when and where to report for the examination. If the location is in a different town or otherwise unfamiliar to you, it would be well to inquire the best route and learn something about the building.
- Relax the night before the test – Allow your mind to rest. Do not study at all that night. Plan some mild recreation or diversion; then go to bed early and get a good night's sleep.
- Get up early enough to make a leisurely trip to the place for the test – This way unforeseen events, traffic snarls, unfamiliar buildings, etc. will not upset you.
- Dress comfortably – A written test is not a fashion show. You will be known by number and not by name, so wear something comfortable.

- Leave excess paraphernalia at home – Shopping bags and odd bundles will get in your way. You need bring only the items mentioned in the official notice you received; usually everything you need is provided. Do not bring reference books to the exam. They will only confuse those last minutes and be taken away from you when in the test room.
- Arrive somewhat ahead of time – If because of transportation schedules you must get there very early, bring a newspaper or magazine to take your mind off yourself while waiting.
- Locate the examination room – When you have found the proper room, you will be directed to the seat or part of the room where you will sit. Sometimes you are given a sheet of instructions to read while you are waiting. Do not fill out any forms until you are told to do so; just read them and be prepared.
- Relax and prepare to listen to the instructions
- If you have any physical problem that may keep you from doing your best, be sure to tell the test administrator. If you are sick or in poor health, you really cannot do your best on the exam. You can come back and take the test some other time.

VII. AT THE TEST

The day of the test is here and you have the test booklet in your hand. The temptation to get going is very strong. Caution! There is more to success than knowing the right answers. You must know how to identify your papers and understand variations in the type of short-answer question used in this particular examination. Follow these suggestions for maximum results from your efforts:

1) Cooperate with the monitor

The test administrator has a duty to create a situation in which you can be as much at ease as possible. He will give instructions, tell you when to begin, check to see that you are marking your answer sheet correctly, and so on. He is not there to guard you, although he will see that your competitors do not take unfair advantage. He wants to help you do your best.

2) Listen to all instructions

Don't jump the gun! Wait until you understand all directions. In most civil service tests you get more time than you need to answer the questions. So don't be in a hurry. Read each word of instructions until you clearly understand the meaning. Study the examples, listen to all announcements and follow directions. Ask questions if you do not understand what to do.

3) Identify your papers

Civil service exams are usually identified by number only. You will be assigned a number; you must not put your name on your test papers. Be sure to copy your number correctly. Since more than one exam may be given, copy your exact examination title.

4) Plan your time

Unless you are told that a test is a "speed" or "rate of work" test, speed itself is usually not important. Time enough to answer all the questions will be provided, but this does not mean that you have all day. An overall time limit has been set. Divide the total time (in minutes) by the number of questions to determine the approximate time you have for each question.

5) Do not linger over difficult questions

If you come across a difficult question, mark it with a paper clip (useful to have along) and come back to it when you have been through the booklet. One caution if you do this – be sure to skip a number on your answer sheet as well. Check often to be sure that you have not lost your place and that you are marking in the row numbered the same as the question you are answering.

6) Read the questions

Be sure you know what the question asks! Many capable people are unsuccessful because they failed to *read* the questions correctly.

7) Answer all questions

Unless you have been instructed that a penalty will be deducted for incorrect answers, it is better to guess than to omit a question.

8) Speed tests

It is often better NOT to guess on speed tests. It has been found that on timed tests people are tempted to spend the last few seconds before time is called in marking answers at random – without even reading them – in the hope of picking up a few extra points. To discourage this practice, the instructions may warn you that your score will be "corrected" for guessing. That is, a penalty will be applied. The incorrect answers will be deducted from the correct ones, or some other penalty formula will be used.

9) Review your answers

If you finish before time is called, go back to the questions you guessed or omitted to give them further thought. Review other answers if you have time.

10) Return your test materials

If you are ready to leave before others have finished or time is called, take ALL your materials to the monitor and leave quietly. Never take any test material with you. The monitor can discover whose papers are not complete, and taking a test booklet may be grounds for disqualification.

VIII. EXAMINATION TECHNIQUES

1) Read the general instructions carefully. These are usually printed on the first page of the exam booklet. As a rule, these instructions refer to the timing of the examination; the fact that you should not start work until the signal and must stop work at a signal, etc. If there are any *special* instructions, such as a choice of questions to be answered, make sure that you note this instruction carefully.

2) When you are ready to start work on the examination, that is as soon as the signal has been given, read the instructions to each question booklet, underline any key words or phrases, such as *least, best, outline, describe* and the like. In this way you will tend to answer as requested rather than discover on reviewing your paper that you *listed without describing*, that you selected the *worst* choice rather than the *best* choice, etc.

3) If the examination is of the objective or multiple-choice type – that is, each question will also give a series of possible answers: A, B, C or D, and you are called upon to select the best answer and write the letter next to that answer on your answer paper – it is advisable to start answering each question in turn. There may be anywhere from 50 to 100 such questions in the three or four hours allotted and you can see how much time would be taken if you read through all the questions before beginning to answer any. Furthermore, if you come across a question or group of questions which you know would be difficult to answer, it would undoubtedly affect your handling of all the other questions.

4) If the examination is of the essay type and contains but a few questions, it is a moot point as to whether you should read all the questions before starting to answer any one. Of course, if you are given a choice – say five out of seven and the like – then it is essential to read all the questions so you can eliminate the two that are most difficult. If, however, you are asked to answer all the questions, there may be danger in trying to answer the easiest one first because you may find that you will spend too much time on it. The best technique is to answer the first question, then proceed to the second, etc.

5) Time your answers. Before the exam begins, write down the time it started, then add the time allowed for the examination and write down the time it must be completed, then divide the time available somewhat as follows:
   - If 3-1/2 hours are allowed, that would be 210 minutes. If you have 80 objective-type questions, that would be an average of 2-1/2 minutes per question. Allow yourself no more than 2 minutes per question, or a total of 160 minutes, which will permit about 50 minutes to review.
   - If for the time allotment of 210 minutes there are 7 essay questions to answer, that would average about 30 minutes a question. Give yourself only 25 minutes per question so that you have about 35 minutes to review.

6) The most important instruction is to *read each question* and make sure you know what is wanted. The second most important instruction is to *time yourself properly* so that you answer every question. The third most important instruction is to *answer every question*. Guess if you have to but include something for each question. Remember that you will receive no credit for a blank and will probably receive some credit if you write something in answer to an essay question. If you guess a letter – say "B" for a multiple-choice question – you may have guessed right. If you leave a blank as an answer to a multiple-choice question, the examiners may respect your feelings but it will not add a point to your score. Some exams may penalize you for wrong answers, so in such cases *only*, you may not want to guess unless you have some basis for your answer.

7) Suggestions
   a. Objective-type questions
      1. Examine the question booklet for proper sequence of pages and questions
      2. Read all instructions carefully
      3. Skip any question which seems too difficult; return to it after all other questions have been answered
      4. Apportion your time properly; do not spend too much time on any single question or group of questions

5. Note and underline key words – *all, most, fewest, least, best, worst, same, opposite,* etc.
6. Pay particular attention to negatives
7. Note unusual option, e.g., unduly long, short, complex, different or similar in content to the body of the question
8. Observe the use of "hedging" words – *probably, may, most likely,* etc.
9. Make sure that your answer is put next to the same number as the question
10. Do not second-guess unless you have good reason to believe the second answer is definitely more correct
11. Cross out original answer if you decide another answer is more accurate; do not erase until you are ready to hand your paper in
12. Answer all questions; guess unless instructed otherwise
13. Leave time for review

b. Essay questions
1. Read each question carefully
2. Determine exactly what is wanted. Underline key words or phrases.
3. Decide on outline or paragraph answer
4. Include many different points and elements unless asked to develop any one or two points or elements
5. Show impartiality by giving pros and cons unless directed to select one side only
6. Make and write down any assumptions you find necessary to answer the questions
7. Watch your English, grammar, punctuation and choice of words
8. Time your answers; don't crowd material

8) Answering the essay question

Most essay questions can be answered by framing the specific response around several key words or ideas. Here are a few such key words or ideas:

M's: manpower, materials, methods, money, management
P's: purpose, program, policy, plan, procedure, practice, problems, pitfalls, personnel, public relations

a. Six basic steps in handling problems:
1. Preliminary plan and background development
2. Collect information, data and facts
3. Analyze and interpret information, data and facts
4. Analyze and develop solutions as well as make recommendations
5. Prepare report and sell recommendations
6. Install recommendations and follow up effectiveness

b. Pitfalls to avoid
1. *Taking things for granted* – A statement of the situation does not necessarily imply that each of the elements is necessarily true; for example, a complaint may be invalid and biased so that all that can be taken for granted is that a complaint has been registered

2. *Considering only one side of a situation* – Wherever possible, indicate several alternatives and then point out the reasons you selected the best one
3. *Failing to indicate follow up* – Whenever your answer indicates action on your part, make certain that you will take proper follow-up action to see how successful your recommendations, procedures or actions turn out to be
4. *Taking too long in answering any single question* – Remember to time your answers properly

IX. AFTER THE TEST

Scoring procedures differ in detail among civil service jurisdictions although the general principles are the same. Whether the papers are hand-scored or graded by machine we have described, they are nearly always graded by number. That is, the person who marks the paper knows only the number – never the name – of the applicant. Not until all the papers have been graded will they be matched with names. If other tests, such as training and experience or oral interview ratings have been given, scores will be combined. Different parts of the examination usually have different weights. For example, the written test might count 60 percent of the final grade, and a rating of training and experience 40 percent. In many jurisdictions, veterans will have a certain number of points added to their grades.

After the final grade has been determined, the names are placed in grade order and an eligible list is established. There are various methods for resolving ties between those who get the same final grade – probably the most common is to place first the name of the person whose application was received first. Job offers are made from the eligible list in the order the names appear on it. You will be notified of your grade and your rank as soon as all these computations have been made. This will be done as rapidly as possible.

People who are found to meet the requirements in the announcement are called "eligibles." Their names are put on a list of eligible candidates. An eligible's chances of getting a job depend on how high he stands on this list and how fast agencies are filling jobs from the list.

When a job is to be filled from a list of eligibles, the agency asks for the names of people on the list of eligibles for that job. When the civil service commission receives this request, it sends to the agency the names of the three people highest on this list. Or, if the job to be filled has specialized requirements, the office sends the agency the names of the top three persons who meet these requirements from the general list.

The appointing officer makes a choice from among the three people whose names were sent to him. If the selected person accepts the appointment, the names of the others are put back on the list to be considered for future openings.

That is the rule in hiring from all kinds of eligible lists, whether they are for typist, carpenter, chemist, or something else. For every vacancy, the appointing officer has his choice of any one of the top three eligibles on the list. This explains why the person whose name is on top of the list sometimes does not get an appointment when some of the persons lower on the list do. If the appointing officer chooses the second or third eligible, the No. 1 eligible does not get a job at once, but stays on the list until he is appointed or the list is terminated.

X. HOW TO PASS THE INTERVIEW TEST

The examination for which you applied requires an oral interview test. You have already taken the written test and you are now being called for the interview test – the final part of the formal examination.

You may think that it is not possible to prepare for an interview test and that there are no procedures to follow during an interview. Our purpose is to point out some things you can do in advance that will help you and some good rules to follow and pitfalls to avoid while you are being interviewed.

What is an interview supposed to test?

The written examination is designed to test the technical knowledge and competence of the candidate; the oral is designed to evaluate intangible qualities, not readily measured otherwise, and to establish a list showing the relative fitness of each candidate – as measured against his competitors – for the position sought. Scoring is not on the basis of "right" and "wrong," but on a sliding scale of values ranging from "not passable" to "outstanding." As a matter of fact, it is possible to achieve a relatively low score without a single "incorrect" answer because of evident weakness in the qualities being measured.

Occasionally, an examination may consist entirely of an oral test – either an individual or a group oral. In such cases, information is sought concerning the technical knowledges and abilities of the candidate, since there has been no written examination for this purpose. More commonly, however, an oral test is used to supplement a written examination.

Who conducts interviews?

The composition of oral boards varies among different jurisdictions. In nearly all, a representative of the personnel department serves as chairman. One of the members of the board may be a representative of the department in which the candidate would work. In some cases, "outside experts" are used, and, frequently, a businessman or some other representative of the general public is asked to serve. Labor and management or other special groups may be represented. The aim is to secure the services of experts in the appropriate field.

However the board is composed, it is a good idea (and not at all improper or unethical) to ascertain in advance of the interview who the members are and what groups they represent. When you are introduced to them, you will have some idea of their backgrounds and interests, and at least you will not stutter and stammer over their names.

What should be done before the interview?

While knowledge about the board members is useful and takes some of the surprise element out of the interview, there is other preparation which is more substantive. It *is* possible to prepare for an oral interview – in several ways:

1) Keep a copy of your application and review it carefully before the interview

This may be the only document before the oral board, and the starting point of the interview. Know what education and experience you have listed there, and the sequence and dates of all of it. Sometimes the board will ask you to review the highlights of your experience for them; you should not have to hem and haw doing it.

2) Study the class specification and the examination announcement

Usually, the oral board has one or both of these to guide them. The qualities, characteristics or knowledges required by the position sought are stated in these documents. They offer valuable clues as to the nature of the oral interview. For example, if the job involves supervisory responsibilities, the announcement will usually indicate that knowledge of modern supervisory methods and the qualifications of the candidate as a supervisor will be tested. If so, you can expect such questions, frequently in the form of a hypothetical situation which you are expected to solve. NEVER go into an oral without knowledge of the duties and responsibilities of the job you seek.

3) Think through each qualification required

Try to visualize the kind of questions you would ask if you were a board member. How well could you answer them? Try especially to appraise your own knowledge and background in each area, *measured against the job sought*, and identify any areas in which you are weak. Be critical and realistic – do not flatter yourself.

4) Do some general reading in areas in which you feel you may be weak

For example, if the job involves supervision and your past experience has NOT, some general reading in supervisory methods and practices, particularly in the field of human relations, might be useful. Do NOT study agency procedures or detailed manuals. The oral board will be testing your understanding and capacity, not your memory.

5) Get a good night's sleep and watch your general health and mental attitude

You will want a clear head at the interview. Take care of a cold or any other minor ailment, and of course, no hangovers.

What should be done on the day of the interview?

Now comes the day of the interview itself. Give yourself plenty of time to get there. Plan to arrive somewhat ahead of the scheduled time, particularly if your appointment is in the fore part of the day. If a previous candidate fails to appear, the board might be ready for you a bit early. By early afternoon an oral board is almost invariably behind schedule if there are many candidates, and you may have to wait. Take along a book or magazine to read, or your application to review, but leave any extraneous material in the waiting room when you go in for your interview. In any event, relax and compose yourself.

The matter of dress is important. The board is forming impressions about you – from your experience, your manners, your attitude, and your appearance. Give your personal appearance careful attention. Dress your best, but not your flashiest. Choose conservative, appropriate clothing, and be sure it is immaculate. This is a business interview, and your appearance should indicate that you regard it as such. Besides, being well groomed and properly dressed will help boost your confidence.

Sooner or later, someone will call your name and escort you into the interview room. *This is it.* From here on you are on your own. It is too late for any more preparation. But remember, you asked for this opportunity to prove your fitness, and you are here because your request was granted.

What happens when you go in?

The usual sequence of events will be as follows: The clerk (who is often the board stenographer) will introduce you to the chairman of the oral board, who will introduce you to the other members of the board. Acknowledge the introductions before you sit down. Do not be surprised if you find a microphone facing you or a stenotypist sitting by. Oral interviews are usually recorded in the event of an appeal or other review.

Usually the chairman of the board will open the interview by reviewing the highlights of your education and work experience from your application – primarily for the benefit of the other members of the board, as well as to get the material into the record. Do not interrupt or comment unless there is an error or significant misinterpretation; if that is the case, do not hesitate. But do not quibble about insignificant matters. Also, he will usually ask you some question about your education, experience or your present job – partly to get you to start talking and to establish the interviewing "rapport." He may start the actual questioning, or turn it over to one of the other members. Frequently, each member undertakes the questioning on a particular area, one in which he is perhaps most competent, so you can expect each member to participate in the examination. Because time is limited, you may also expect some rather abrupt switches in the direction the questioning takes, so do not be upset by it. Normally, a board member will not pursue a single line of questioning unless he discovers a particular strength or weakness.

After each member has participated, the chairman will usually ask whether any member has any further questions, then will ask you if you have anything you wish to add. Unless you are expecting this question, it may floor you. Worse, it may start you off on an extended, extemporaneous speech. The board is not usually seeking more information. The question is principally to offer you a last opportunity to present further qualifications or to indicate that you have nothing to add. So, if you feel that a significant qualification or characteristic has been overlooked, it is proper to point it out in a sentence or so. Do not compliment the board on the thoroughness of their examination – they have been sketchy, and you know it. If you wish, merely say, "No thank you, I have nothing further to add." This is a point where you can "talk yourself out" of a good impression or fail to present an important bit of information. Remember, *you close the interview yourself.*

The chairman will then say, "That is all, Mr. _____, thank you." Do not be startled; the interview is over, and quicker than you think. Thank him, gather your belongings and take your leave. Save your sigh of relief for the other side of the door.

How to put your best foot forward
Throughout this entire process, you may feel that the board individually and collectively is trying to pierce your defenses, seek out your hidden weaknesses and embarrass and confuse you. Actually, this is not true. They are obliged to make an appraisal of your qualifications for the job you are seeking, and they want to see you in your best light. Remember, they must interview all candidates and a non-cooperative candidate may become a failure in spite of their best efforts to bring out his qualifications. Here are 15 suggestions that will help you:

1) Be natural – Keep your attitude confident, not cocky
If you are not confident that you can do the job, do not expect the board to be. Do not apologize for your weaknesses, try to bring out your strong points. The board is interested in a positive, not negative, presentation. Cockiness will antagonize any board member and make him wonder if you are covering up a weakness by a false show of strength.

2) Get comfortable, but don't lounge or sprawl
Sit erectly but not stiffly. A careless posture may lead the board to conclude that you are careless in other things, or at least that you are not impressed by the importance of the occasion. Either conclusion is natural, even if incorrect. Do not fuss with your clothing, a pencil or an ashtray. Your hands may occasionally be useful to emphasize a point; do not let them become a point of distraction.

3) Do not wisecrack or make small talk
This is a serious situation, and your attitude should show that you consider it as such. Further, the time of the board is limited – they do not want to waste it, and neither should you.

4) Do not exaggerate your experience or abilities

In the first place, from information in the application or other interviews and sources, the board may know more about you than you think. Secondly, you probably will not get away with it. An experienced board is rather adept at spotting such a situation, so do not take the chance.

5) If you know a board member, do not make a point of it, yet do not hide it

Certainly you are not fooling him, and probably not the other members of the board. Do not try to take advantage of your acquaintanceship – it will probably do you little good.

6) Do not dominate the interview

Let the board do that. They will give you the clues – do not assume that you have to do all the talking. Realize that the board has a number of questions to ask you, and do not try to take up all the interview time by showing off your extensive knowledge of the answer to the first one.

7) Be attentive

You only have 20 minutes or so, and you should keep your attention at its sharpest throughout. When a member is addressing a problem or question to you, give him your undivided attention. Address your reply principally to him, but do not exclude the other board members.

8) Do not interrupt

A board member may be stating a problem for you to analyze. He will ask you a question when the time comes. Let him state the problem, and wait for the question.

9) Make sure you understand the question

Do not try to answer until you are sure what the question is. If it is not clear, restate it in your own words or ask the board member to clarify it for you. However, do not haggle about minor elements.

10) Reply promptly but not hastily

A common entry on oral board rating sheets is "candidate responded readily," or "candidate hesitated in replies." Respond as promptly and quickly as you can, but do not jump to a hasty, ill-considered answer.

11) Do not be peremptory in your answers

A brief answer is proper – but do not fire your answer back. That is a losing game from your point of view. The board member can probably ask questions much faster than you can answer them.

12) Do not try to create the answer you think the board member wants

He is interested in what kind of mind you have and how it works – not in playing games. Furthermore, he can usually spot this practice and will actually grade you down on it.

13) Do not switch sides in your reply merely to agree with a board member

Frequently, a member will take a contrary position merely to draw you out and to see if you are willing and able to defend your point of view. Do not start a debate, yet do not surrender a good position. If a position is worth taking, it is worth defending.

14) Do not be afraid to admit an error in judgment if you are shown to be wrong

The board knows that you are forced to reply without any opportunity for careful consideration. Your answer may be demonstrably wrong. If so, admit it and get on with the interview.

15) Do not dwell at length on your present job

The opening question may relate to your present assignment. Answer the question but do not go into an extended discussion. You are being examined for a *new* job, not your present one. As a matter of fact, try to phrase ALL your answers in terms of the job for which you are being examined.

Basis of Rating

Probably you will forget most of these "do's" and "don'ts" when you walk into the oral interview room. Even remembering them all will not ensure you a passing grade. Perhaps you did not have the qualifications in the first place. But remembering them will help you to put your best foot forward, without treading on the toes of the board members.

Rumor and popular opinion to the contrary notwithstanding, an oral board wants you to make the best appearance possible. They know you are under pressure – but they also want to see how you respond to it as a guide to what your reaction would be under the pressures of the job you seek. They will be influenced by the degree of poise you display, the personal traits you show and the manner in which you respond.

ABOUT THIS BOOK

This book contains tests divided into Examination Sections. Go through each test, answering every question in the margin. We have also attached a sample answer sheet at the back of the book that can be removed and used. At the end of each test look at the answer key and check your answers. On the ones you got wrong, look at the right answer choice and learn. Do not fill in the answers first. Do not memorize the questions and answers, but understand the answer and principles involved. On your test, the questions will likely be different from the samples. Questions are changed and new ones added. If you understand these past questions you should have success with any changes that arise. Tests may consist of several types of questions. We have additional books on each subject should more study be advisable or necessary for you. Finally, the more you study, the better prepared you will be. This book is intended to be the last thing you study before you walk into the examination room. Prior study of relevant texts is also recommended. NLC publishes some of these in our Fundamental Series. Knowledge and good sense are important factors in passing your exam. Good luck also helps. So now study this Passbook, absorb the material contained within and take that knowledge into the examination. Then do your best to pass that exam.

EXAMINATION SECTION

EXAMINATION SECTION
TEST 1

DIRECTIONS: Each question or incomplete statement is followed by several suggested answers or completions. Select the one that BEST answers the question or completes the statement. *PRINT THE LETTER OF THE CORRECT ANSWER IN THE SPACE AT THE RIGHT.*

1. If you open a personal letter by mistake, the one of the following actions which it would generall be BEST for u to take is to

    A. ignore your error, attach the envelope to the letter, and distribute in the usual manner
    B. personally give the addressee the letter without any explanation
    C. place the letter inside the envelope, indicate under your initials that it was opened in error, and give to the addressee
    D. reseal the envelope or place the contents in another envelope and pass on to addressee

    1.____

2. If you receive a telephone call regarding a matter which your office does not handle, you should FIRST

    A. give the caller the telephone number of the proper office so that he can dial again
    B. offer to transfer the caller to the proper office
    C. suggest that the caller re-dial since he probably dialed incorrectly
    D. tell the caller he has reached the wrong office and then hang up

    2.____

3. When you answer the telephone, the MOST important reason for identifying yourself and your organization is to

    A. give the caller time to collect his or her thoughts
    B. impress the caller with your courtesy
    C. inform the caller that he or she has reached the right number
    D. set a business-like tone at the beginning of the conversatio

    3.____

4. The one of the following cases in which you would NOT place a special notation in the left margin of a letter that you have typed is when

    A. one of the copies is intended for someone other than the addressee of the letter
    B. you enclose a flyer with the letter
    C. you sign your superior's name to the letter at his or her request
    D. the letter refers to something being sent under separate cover

    4.____

5. Suppose that you accidentally cut a letter or enclosure as you are opening an envelope with a paper knife.
The one of the following that you should do FIRST is to

    A. determine whether the document is important
    B. clip or staple the pieces together and process as usual
    C. mend the cut document with transparent tape
    D. notify the sender that the communication was damaged and request another copy

    5.____

1

6. It is generally advisable to leave at least six inches of working space in a file drawer. This procedure is MOST useful in

   A. decreasing the number of filing errors
   B. facilitating the sorting of documents and folders
   C. maintaining a regular program of removing inactive records
   D. preventing folders and papers from being torn

7. Of the following, the MOST important reason to sort large volumes of documents before filing is that sorting

   A. decreases the need for cross-referencing
   B. eliminates the need to keep the files up to date
   C. prevents overcrowding of the file drawers
   D. saves time and energy in filing

8. When typing a preliminary draft of a report, the one of the following which you should generally NOT do is to

   A. erase typing errors and deletions rather than *x*-ing them out
   B. leave plenty of room at the top, bottom and sides of each page
   C. make only the number of copies that you are asked to make
   D. type double or triple space

9. The BEST way for a receptionist to deal with a situation in which she must leave her desk for a long time is to

   A. ask someone to take her place while she is away
   B. leave a note or sign on her desk which indicates the time she will return
   C. take a chance that no one will arrive while she is gone and leave her desk unattended
   D. tell a co-worker to ask any visitors that arrive to wait until she returns

10. Suppose that two individuals come up to your desk at the same time. One of them asks you for the location of the nearest public phone. After you answer the question, you turn to the second person who asks you the same question. The one of the following actions which it would be BEST for you to take in this situation is to

    A. ignore the second person since he obviously overheard your first answer
    B. point out that you just answered the same question and quickly repeat the information
    C. politely repeat the information to the second individual
    D. tell the second person to follow the first to the public telephone

11. Suppose that you are newly assigned to a large office in your department. You believe that a certain change in office routine would be desirable.
    Of the following, the BEST reason for suggesting this modification to your supervisor is that

    A. even good supervisors are sometimes reluctant to institute innovations
    B. your suggestion may result in the saving of considerable time and money
    C. major changes in office routine are easier to make in small offices than in large offices
    D. a new employee will usually be able to think of new ways of doing his work

12. When typing names or titles on a roll of folder labels, the one of the following which it is MOST important to do is to type the caption 12.____

    A. as it appears on the papers to be placed in the folder
    B. in capital letters
    C. in exact indexing or filing order
    D. so that it appears near the bottom of the folder tab when the label is attached

Questions 13-17.

DIRECTIONS: Questions 13 through 17 consist of the names of students who have applied for a certain college program and are to be classified according to the criteria described below.

The following table gives pertinent data for 6 different applicants with regard to:
Grade averages, which are expressed on a scale running from
    0 (low) to 4 (high);
Scores on qualifying test, which run from 200 (low) to 800 (high); Related work experience, which is expressed in number of months; Personal references, which are rated from 1 (low) to 5 (high).

Applicant	Grade Average	Test Score	Work Experience	Reference
Jones	2.2	620	24	3
Perez	3.5	650	0	5
Lowitz	3.2	420	2	4
Uncker	2.1	710	15	2
Farrow	2.8	560	0	3
Shapiro	3.0	560	12	4

An administrative assistant is in charge of the initial screening process for the program. This process requires classifying applicants into the following four groups:

A. SUPERIOR CANDIDATES. Unless the personal reference rating is lower than 3, all applicants with grade averages of 3.0 or higher and test scores of 600 or higher are classified as superior candidates.
B. GOOD CANDIDATES. Unless the personal reference rating is lower than 3, all applicants with one of the following combinations of grade averages and test scores are classified as good candidates: (1) grade average of 2.5 to 2.9 and test score of 600 or higher; (2) grade average of 3.0 or higher and test score of 550 to 599.
C. POSSIBLE CANDIDATES. Applicants with one of the following combinations of qualifications are classified as possible candidates: (1) grade average of 2.5 to 2.9 and test score of 550 to 599 and a personal reference rating of 3 or higher; (2) grade average of 2.0 to 2.4 and test score of 500 or higher and at least 21 months' work experience and a personal reference rating of 3 or higher; (3) a combination of grade average and test score that would otherwise qualify as *superior* or *good* but a personal reference score lower than 3.
D. REJECTED CANDIDATES. Applicants who do not fall in any of the above groups are to be rejected.

EXAMPLE

Jones' grade average of 2.2 does not meet the standard for either a superior candidate (grade average must be 3.0 or higher) or a good candidate (grade average must be 2.5 to 2.9). Grade average of 2.2 does not qualify Jones as a possible candidate if Jones has a test score of 500 or higher, at least 21 months' work experience, and a personal reference rating of 3 or higher. Since Jones has a test score of 620, 24 months' work experience, and a reference rating of 3, Jones is a possible candidate. The answer is C.

Answer Questions 13 through 17 as explained above, indicating for each whether the applicant should be classified as a

    A. superior candidate   B. good candidate
    C. possible candidate   D. rejected candidate

13. Perez
14. Lowitz
15. Uncker
16. Farrow
17. Shapiro

18. An *attention* line is used in correspondence to

    A. indicate to the person receiving the correspondence that it contains an enclosure
    B. direct correspondence addressed to an organization to a particular individual within the organization
    C. greet the recipient of the correspondence
    D. highlight the main concern of the correspondence

19. The MOST important reason for a person in charge of a petty cash fund to obtain receipts for payments is that this practice would tend to

    A. decrease robberies by delivery personnel
    B. eliminate the need to keep a record of petty cash expenditures
    C. prove that the fund has been used properly
    D. provide a record of the need for cash in the daily operations of the office

20. You should generally replenish a petty cash fund

    A. at regularly established intervals
    B. each time you withdraw a sum of more than $2.00
    C. when the amount of cash gets below a certain specified amount
    D. when the fund is completely empty

Questions 21-32.

DIRECTIONS: In Questions 21 through 32, choose the lettered word which means MOST NEARLY the same as the italicized word in the sentence.

21. The aims of the students and the aims of the faculty often *coincide*.

    A. agree   B. are ignored
    C. conflict   D. are misinterpreted

22. The secretary of the sociology department was responsible for setting up an index of *relevant* magazine articles.

    A. applicable   B. controversial
    C. miscellaneous   D. recent

23. One of the secretary's duties consisted of sorting and filing *facsimiles* of student term papers.   23.____

    A. bibliographical listings B. exact copies
    C. summaries D. supporting documentation

24. *Stringent* requirements for advanced physics courses often result in small class sizes.   24.____

    A. lengthy B. remarkable C. rigid D. vague

25. The professor explained that the report was too *verbose* to be submitted.   25.____

    A. brief B. specific C. general D. wordy

26. The faculty meeting *pre-empted* the conference room in the Dean's office.   26.____

    A. appropriated B. emptied
    C. filled D. reserved

27. The professor's credentials became a subject of *controversy*.   27.____

    A. annoyance B. debate C. envy D. review

28. The professor developed a different central theme during every *semester*   28.____

    A. bi-annual period of instruction
    B. orientation period
    C. slide demonstration
    D. weekly lecture series

29. The college offered a variety of *seminars* to upperclassmen.   29.____

    A. reading courses with no formal supervision
    B. study courses for small groups of students engaged
    C. in research under a teacher
    D. guidance conferences with grade advisors
    E. work experiences in different occupational fields

30. The Dean pointed out that the *focus* of the study was not clear.   30.____

    A. end B. objective C. follow-up D. location

31. The faculty of the anthropology department agreed that the departmental program was *deficient*.   31.____

    A. excellent B. inadequate C. demanding D. sufficien

32. The secretary was asked to type a rough draft of a college course *syllabus*.   32.____

    A. directory of departments and services
    B. examination schedule
    C. outline of a course of study
    D. rules and regulations

Questions 33-40.

DIRECTIONS: Each of the questions numbered 33 through 40 consists of three sets of names and name codes. In each question, the two names and name codes on the same line are supposed to be exactly the same.

Look carefully at each set of names and codes and mark your answer
A. if there are mistakes in all three sets
B. if there are mistakes in two of the sets
C. if there is a mistake in only one set
D. if there are no mistakes in any of the sets

SAMPLE QUESTION

The following sample question is given to help you understand the procedure:

Macabe, John N.- V 53162 Macade, John N.- V 53162
Howard, Joan S.- J 24791 Howard, Joan S. - J 24791
Ware, Susan B. - A 45068 Ware, Susan B. - A45968

In the above sample question, the names and name codes of the first set are not exactly the same because of the spelling of the last name (Macabe - Macade). The names and name codes of the second set are exactly the same.

The names and name codes of the third set are not exactly the same because the two name codes are different (A 45068 - A 45968). Since there are mistakes in only two of the sets, the answer to the sample question is B.

33. Powell, Michael C. - 78537 F Powell, Michael C. - 78537 F
    Martinez, Pablo J. - 24435 P Martinez, Pablo J. - 24435 P
    MacBane, Eliot M. - 98674 E MacBane, Eliot M. - 98674 E

34. Fitz-Kramer Machines Inc. - 259090 Fitz-Kramer Machines Inc. - 259090
    Marvel Cleaning Service - 482657 Marvel Cleaning Service - 482657
    Donato, Carl G. - 637418 Danato, Carl G. - 687418

35. Martin Davison Trading Corp.- 43108 T Martin Davidson Trading Corp. - 43108 T
    Cotwald Lighting Fixtures - 70056 L Cotwald Lighting Fixtures - 76065 L
    R. Crawford Plumbers - 23157 G R. Crawford Plumbers - 23157 C

36. Fraiman Engineering Corp.- M4773 Friaman Engineering Corp. - M4773
    Neuman, Walter B. - N7745 Neumen, Walter B. - N7745
    Pierce, Eric M. - W6304 Pierce, Eric M. - W6304

37. Constable, Eugene - B 64837 Comstable, Eugene - B 64837
    Derrick, Paul - H 27119 Derrik, Paul - H 27119
    Heller, Karen - S 49606 Heller, Karen - S 46906

38. Hernando Delivery Service Co. Hernando Delivery Service Co.
    - D 7456 - D 7456
    Barettz Electrical Supplies - N 5392 Barettz Electrical Supplies - N 5392
    Tanner, Abraham - M 4798 Tanner, Abraham - M 4798

39. Kalin Associates - R 38641 Kaline Associates - R 38641
    Sealey, Robert E. - P 63533 Sealey, Robert E. - P 63553
    Scalsi Office Furniture - R 36742 Scalsi Office Furniture - R 36742

40. Janowsky, Philip M. - 742213 Janowsky, Philip M. - 742213
    Hansen, Thomas H. - 934816 Hanson, Thomas H. - 934816
    L. Lester and Son Inc. - 294568 L. Lester and Son Inc. - 294568

KEY (CORRECT ANSWERS)

1.	C	11.	B	21.	A	31.	B
2.	B	12.	C	22.	A	32.	C
3.	C	13.	A	23.	B	33.	D
4.	C	14.	D	24.	C	34.	C
5.	C	15.	D	25.	D	35.	A
6.	D	16.	C	26.	A	36.	B
7.	D	17.	B	27.	B	37.	A
8.	A	18.	B	28.	A	38.	D
9.	A	19.	C	29.	B	39.	B
10.	C	20.	C	30.	B	40.	C

TEST 2

DIRECTIONS: Each question or incomplete statement is followed by several suggested answers or completions. Select the one that BEST answers the question or completes the statement. *PRINT THE LETTER OF THE CORRECT ANSWER IN THE SPACE AT THE RIGHT.*

1. When you determine the methods of emphasis you will use in typing the titles, headings, and subheadings of a report, the one of the following which it is MOST important to keep in mind is that 1.___

    A. all headings of the same rank should be typed in the same way
    B. all headings should be typed in the single style which is most pleasing to the eye
    C. headings should not take up more than one-third of the page width
    D. only one method should be used for all headings, whatever their rank

2. After checking several times, you are unable to locate a student record in its proper file drawer. The file drawer in question is used constantly by many members of the staff. In this situation, the NEXT step you should take in locating the missing record is to 2.___

    A. ask another worker to look through the file drawer
    B. determine if there is another copy of the record filed in a different place
    C. find out if the record has been removed by another staff member
    D. wait a day or two and see if the record turns up

3. It is MOST important that an enclosure which is to be mailed with a letter should be put in an envelope so that 3.___

    A. any printing on the enclosure will not be visible through the address side of the envelope
    B. it is obvious that there is an enclosure inside the envelope
    C. the enclosure takes up less space than the letter
    D. the person who opens the envelope will put out both the letter and the enclosure

4. Suppose that one of the student aides with whom you work suggests a change in the filing procedure. He is sure the change will result in increased rates of filing among the other employees.
The one of the following which you should do FIRST is to 4.___

    A. ask him to demonstrate his method in order to determine if he files more quickly than the other employees
    B. ask your supervisor if you may make a change in the filing procedure
    C. ignore the aide's suggestion since he is not a filing expert
    D. tell him to show his method to the other employees and to encourage them to use it

5. When opening mail by hand, the one of the following methods which would generally be BEST to use is to 5.___

    A. cut off one end of the envelope
    B. cut off the top of the envelope
    C. place the envelope face down on your desk and pull the flap of the envelope back
    D. place the envelope face down on your desk and run a sharp flat instrument under the flap

6. Suppose that the chairman of a program in a senior college where you work has asked you for the entire file folder on a particular student in the program.
Since he tells you that he may have the folder out for some time, it would generally be BEST for you to

   A. make a copy of each document in the folder, prepare a new folder, and place it in the file
   B. place an out folder in the file
   C. place a cross-reference card in the file
   D. place a slip of paper in the file indicating why the folder was removed

6._____

7. The one of the following ways in which inter-office memoranda differ from long formal reports is that they GENERALLY

   A. are written as if the reader is familiar with the vocabulary and technical background of the writer
   B. do not have a *subject line* which describes the major topic covered in the text
   C. include a listing of reference materials which support the memo writer's conclusions
   D. require that a letter of transmittal be attached

7._____

Questions 8-15.

DIRECTIONS: Each Question 8 through 15 consists of four names. For each question, choose the one of the four names that should be LAST if the four names were arranged in alphabetical order in accordance with the RULES FOR ALPHABETICAL FILING given below. Read these rules carefully. Then, for each question, indicate in the numbered space at the right the letter before the name that should be LAST in alphabetical order.

RULES FOR ALPHABETICAL FILING

Names of Individuals.

1. *The names of individuals are filed in strict alphabetical order, first according to the last name, then according to first name or initial, and finally according to middle name or initial. For example: George Allen comes before Edward Bell, and Leonard P. Reston comes before Lucille B. Reston.*

2. *When last names are the same, for example, A. Green and Agnes Green, the one with the initial comes before the one with the name written out when the first initials are identical.*

3. *When first and last names are alike, the name without a middle initial comes before the one with a middle name or initial. For example: John Doe comes before both John A. Doe and John Alan Doe.*

4. *When first and last names are the same, the name with a middle initial comes before the one with a middle name beginning with the same initial. For example: Jack R. Herts comes before Jack Richard Hertz.*

5. Prefixes such as De, O', Mac, Mc, and Van are filed as written and are treated as part of the names they come before. For example: Robert O'Dea is filed before David Olsen.

6. Abbreviated names are treated as if they were spelled out. For example: Chas. is filed as Charles, and Thos. is filed as Thomas.

7. Titles and designations such as Dr., Mr., and Prof, are disregarded in filing.

<u>Names of Business Organizations.</u>

1. The names of business organizations are filed according to the order in which each word in the name appears. When an organization name bears the name of a person, it is filed according to the rules for filing names of people as given above. For example: William Smith Service Co. comes before Television Distributors, Inc.

2. When the following words are part of a business name, they are disregarded: the, of, and.

3. When there are numbers in a name, they are treated as if they were spelled out. For example: 10th Street Bootery is filed as Tenth Street Bootery.

<u>Names of Government Offices</u>

Bureaus, boards, offices, and departments of the city government are filed under the name of the chief governing body. For example: Bureau of the Budget would be filed as if written Budget (Bureau of the).

SAMPLE QUESTION:
- A. Jane Earl (2)
- B. James A. Earle (4)
- C. James Earl (1)
- D. J. Earle (3)

The numbers in parentheses show the proper alphabetical order in which these names should be filed. Since the name that should be filed LAST is James A. Earle, the answer to the Sample Question is B.

8.
- A. Corral, Dr. Robert
- B. Carrale, Prof. Robert
- C. Corren, R.
- D. Corret, Ron

9.
- A. Rivera, Ilena
- B. Riviera, Ilene
- C. Rivere, I.
- D. Riviera Ice-Cream Co.

10.
- A. VonHogel, George
- B. Volper, Gary
- C. Vonner, G.
- D. Van Pefel, Gregory

11. A. David Kallish Stationery Co.
     B. Emerson Microfilm Company
     C. David Kalder Industrial Engineers Associated
     D. 5th Avenue Office Furniture Co.

11.____

12. A. Bennet, C.
     B. Benett, Chuck
     C. Bennet, Chas.
     D. Bennett, Charles

12.____

13. A. The Board of Higher Education
     A. National Education Commission
     B. Eakin, Hugh
     C. Nathan, Ellen

13.____

14. A. McCloud, I.
     B. MacGowen, Ian
     C. McGowen, Arthur
     D. Macale, Sean

14.____

15. A. Devine, Sarah
     B. Devine, S.
     C. Devine, Sara H.
     D. Devin, Sarah

15.____

Questions 16-21.

DIRECTIONS: Answer Questions 16 through 21 SOLELY on the basis of the following paragraphs.

A folder is made of a sheet of heavy paper (manila, kraft, press-board, or red rope stock) that has been folded once so that the back is about one-half inch higher than the front. Folders are larger than the papers they contain in order to protect them. Two standard folder sizes are "letter size" for papers that are 8 1/2" x 11" and "legal cap" for papers that are 8 1/2" x 13".

Folders are cut across the top in two ways: so that the back is straight (straight-cut), or so that the back has a tab that projects above the top of the folder. Such tabs bear captions that identify the contents of each folder. Tabs vary in width and position. The tabs of a set of folders that are "one-half cut" are half the width of the folder, and have only two positions.

"One-third cut" folders have three positions, each tab occupying a third of the width of the folder. Another standard tabbing is "one-fifth cut," which has five positions. There are also folders with "two-fifths cut," with the tabs in the third and fourth, or fourth and fifth, positions.

16. Of the following, the BEST title for the above passage is

16.____

| A. Filing Folders | B. Standard Folder Sizes |
| C. The Uses of the Folder | D. The Use of Tabs |

17. According to the above passage, one of the standard folder sizes is called

   A. kraft cut
   B. legal cap
   C. one-half cut
   D. straight-cut

18. According to the above passage, tabs are GENERALLY placed along the _____ of the folder.

   A. back
   B. front
   C. left side
   D. right side

19. According to the above passage, a tab is GENERALLY used to

   A. distinguish between standard folder sizes
   B. identify the contents of a folder
   C. increase the size of the folder
   D. protect the papers within the folder

20. According to the above passage, a folder that is two-fifths cut has _____ tabs.

   A. no   B. two   C. three   D. five

21. According to the above passage, one reason for making folders larger than the papers they contain is that

   A. only a certain size folder can be made from heavy paper
   B. they will protect the papers
   C. they will aid in setting up a tab system
   D. the back of the folder must be higher than the front

Questions 22-30.

DIRECTIONS: Answer Questions 22 through 30 SOLELY on the basis of the following paragraphs.

The City University of New York traces its origins to 1847, when the Free Academy, which later became City College, was founded as the first tuition-free municipal college. City and Hunter Colleges were placed under the direction of the Board of Higher Education in 1926, and Brooklyn and Queens Colleges were subsequently added to the system of municipal colleges. In 1955, Staten Island Community College, the first of the two-year colleges sponsored by the Board of Higher Education under the program of the State University of flew York, joined the system.

In 1961, the four senior colleges and three community colleges then under the jurisdiction of the Board of Higher Education became the City University of New York, and a University Graduate Division was organized to offer programs leading to the Ph.D. Since then, the university has undergone even more rapid growth. Today it consists of nine senior colleges, an upper division college which admits students at the junior level, eight community colleges, a graduate division, and an affiliated medical center.

In the summer of 1969, the Board of Higher Education resolved that the time had come to commit the resources of the university to meeting an urgent social need -- unrestricted access to higher education for all youths of the City. Determined to prevent the waste of human potential represented by the thousands of high school graduates whose limited educational opportunities left them unable to meet existing admission standards, the Board moved to adopt a policy of Open Admissions. It was their judgment that the best way of determining whether a potential student can benefit from college work is to admit him to college, provide him with the learning assistance he needs, and then evaluate his performance.

Beginning with the class of June 1970, every New York City resident who receives a high school diploma from a public or private high school is guaranteed a place in one of the colleges of City University.

22. Of the following, the BEST title for the above passage is

    A. A Brief History of the City University
    B. High Schools and the City University
    C. The Components of the University
    D. Tuition-Free Colleges

23. According to the above passage, the one of the following colleges of the City University which was ORIGINALLY called the Free Academy was _____ College.

    A. Brooklyn   B. City   C. Hunter   D. Queens

24. According to the above passage, the system of municipal colleges became the City University of New York in

    A. 1926   B. 1955   C. 1961   D. 1969

25. According to the above passage, Staten Island Community College came under the jurisdiction of the Board of Higher Education

    A. 6 years after a Graduate Division was organized
    B. 8 years before the adoption of the Open Admissions Policy
    C. 29 years after Brooklyn and Queens Colleges
    D. 29 years after City and Hunter Colleges

26. According to the above passage, the Staten Island Community College is a(n)

    A. graduate division center   B. senior college
    C. two-year college   D. upper division college

27. According to the above passage, the TOTAL number of colleges, divisions, and affiliated branches of the City University is

    A. 18   B. 19   C. 20   D. 21

28. According to the above passage, the open admissions policy is designed to determine whether a potential student will benefit from college by PRIMARILY

    A. discouraging competition for placement in the City University among high school students
    B. evaluating his performance after entry into college

C. lowering admission standards
D. providing learning assistance before entry into college

29. According to the above passage, the FIRST class to be affected by the open admissions policy was the

   A. high school class which graduated in January 1970
   B. City University class which graduated in June 1970
   C. high school class which graduated in June 1970
   D. City University class which graduated in January 1970

30. According to the above passage, one of the reasons that the Board of Higher Education initiated the policy of open admissions was to

   A. enable high school graduates with a background of limited educational opportunities to enter college
   B. expand the growth of the City University so as to increase the number and variety of degrees offered
   C. provide a social resource to the qualified youth of the City
   D. revise admission standards to meet the needs of the City

Questions 31-37.

DIRECTIONS: Answer Questions 31 through 37 SOLELY on the basis of the table below referring to agency Part-time employees.

| Emp. No. | Name | Exempt. | Gross Earnings | Deductions | | | | | Total Deductions | Net Earnings |
				Fed. With. Tax	FICA	Grp. Ins	Hosp.	Bonds		
123	Anderson, Paul	1	72.50	7.90	3.64	.85	.95		13.34	59.16
209	Greene, Henry	4	85.00	4.00	2.52	.85	.95		8.32	76.68
27	Kowalski, Anna	2	158.33	17.30	8.03	.97	1.10		27.50	130.83
174	Rodriguez, Marie	1	85.00	7.45	2.52	.80	.95		11.72	73.28
362	Rosen, Carl	2	112.28	12.40	5.48	.80	.95		19.63	92.65
198	Sung, Wang Y.	3	95.00	6.00	3.77	.93	1.05	2.00	13.75	81.25
53	Tomasso, Francis	4	190.81	18.60	8.56	1.12	1.20	3.00	32.48	158.33
	Total		798.92	73.65	34.62	6.32	7.15	5.00	126.74	672.18

31. According to the above chart, the sum of the total deductions is APPROXIMATELY what percent of the total gross earnings?

   A. 6.3%   B. 9.3%   C. 15.8%   D. 18.6%

32. According to the above chart, the sum of the net earnings of two of the employees is MOST NEARLY the same as the gross earnings of the employee named   32._____

   A. Anna Kowalski   B. Carl Rosen
   C. Henry Greene   D. Wang Y. Sung

33. According to the above chart, the AVERAGE amount deducted for Federal withholding tax of all employees with gross earnings over $100 is   33._____

   A. $5.55   B. $6.33   C. $16.10   D. $17.95

34. According to the above chart, the AVERAGE net earnings for all employees with net earnings below $100 is *approximately*   34._____

   A. $67.34   B. $76.60   C. $84.38   D. $96.20

35. According to the above chart, the employee who has the HIGHEST percent of his or her gross earnings deducted is   35._____

   A. Paul Anderson   B. Henry Greene
   C. Anna Kowalski   D. Carl Rosen

36. According to the above chart, the number of employees whose Federal withholding tax is GREATER than 10% of their gross earnings is   36._____

   A. 2   B. 3   C. 4   D. 5

37. According to the above chart, the net earnings of one employee are equal to the gross earnings of another employee.   37._____
   The TWO employees about whom this statement can be made are:

   A. Marie Rodriguez and Carl Rosen
   B. Paul Anderson and Henry Greene
   C. Henry Greene and Marie Rodriguez
   D. Anna Kowalski and Francis Tomasso

38. You are preparing a package of six books to mail to a professor who is on sabbatical. They weigh, respectively, 1 pound 11 ounces, 1 pound 6 ounces, 2 pounds 1 ounce, 2 pounds 2 ounces, 1 pound 7 ounces, and 1 pound 8 ounces. The packaging material weighs 6 ounces.   38._____
   The TOTAL weight of the package will be _____ pounds _____ ounces.

   A. 10; 3   B. 10; 9   C. 11; 5   D. 12; 5

39. Part-time students are charged $35.00 per credit for courses at a particular college. In addition, they must pay a $12.00 student activity fee if they take six credits or more and a $7.00 lab fee for each laboratory course.   39._____
   If a person takes one 3-credit course and one 4-credit course and his 4-credit course is a laboratory course, the TOTAL cost to him will be

   A. $252.00   B. $264.00   C. $271.00   D. $276.00

40. The graduating class of a certain community college consisted of 378 majors in secretarial science, 265 majors in engineering science, 57 majors in nursing, 513 majors in accounting, and 865 majors in liberal arts. The percent of students who major in liberal arts at this college was MOST NEARLY

 A. 24.0%   B. 41.6%   C. 52.3%   D. 71.6%

KEY (CORRECT ANSWERS)

1.	A	11.	A	21.	B	31.	C
2.	C	12.	D	22.	A	32.	A
3.	D	13.	B	23.	B	33.	C
4.	A	14.	C	24.	C	34.	B
5.	D	15.	A	25.	B	35.	A
6.	B	16.	A	26.	C	36.	B
7.	A	17.	B	27.	C	37.	D
8.	D	18.	A	28.	B	38.	B
9.	B	19.	B	29.	C	39.	B
10.	C	20.	B	30.	A	40.	B

EXAMINATION SECTION
TEST 1

DIRECTIONS: Each question or incomplete statement is followed by several suggested answers or completions. Select the one that BEST answers the question or completes the statement. *PRINT THE LETTER OF THE CORRECT ANSWER IN THE SPACE AT THE RIGHT.*

Questions 1-2.

DIRECTIONS: Questions 1 and 2 are based on the following paragraph.

Screening interviews and selection interviews serve two separate and distinct purposes. Accordingly, the types of questions asked in each should tend to relate to these purposes.

1. Of the following, the question MOST appropriate for initial screening purposes generally is:

    A. What are your salary requirements?
    B. Why do you think you would like this kind of work?
    C. How did you get along with your last supervisor?
    D. What are your vocational goals?

2. Of the following, *normally* the question MOST appropriate for selection purposes generally would tend to be:

    A. Where did you work last?
    B. When did you graduate from high school?
    C. What was your average in school?
    D. Why did you select this organization?

3. When making formal business introductions between a man and a woman in official positions, the one of the following which is considered *proper* practice is, MOST generally, to present the

    A. man to the woman when the man has superior rank
    B. man to the woman when the woman has superior rank
    C. man to the woman when the woman is older but of lower rank
    D. woman to the man when their ranks are equal

4. While training a group of new student aides, an office assistant notices that one of them is not paying attention. Of the following, the MOST appropriate method for the office assistant to use in order to properly sustain attention and maintain discipline would GENERALLY be for her to

    A. reprimand the aide immediately in front of the group
    B. call a break period and then privately find out why this aide is not paying attention
    C. ask the aide to leave the training area until she has a chance to speak to him
    D. ignore the aide's behavior since the aide will be the one who will suffer later on

5. While you are working as an office assistant in the Registrar's Office, a student comes to you with a problem. Two weeks earlier, he requested that his transcript be sent to a graduate school, but at this time, it still hasn't been received by the graduate school. While speaking to you, the student becomes sarcastic and argumentative.
Of the following, it *normally* would be BEST for you to

   A. tell the student to leave the Registrar's Office and not to return for at least two days
   B. begin to treat the student in a similar manner in order to show him what his behavior is like
   C. remain calm and check to determine what has happened to the student's request
   D. treat the student politely and give him a complimentary photocopy of his transcript so that he can send it special delivery

5.____

Questions 6-15.

DIRECTIONS: Each statement in Questions 6 through 15 contains one of the faults of English usage listed below. For each, choose from the options listed the MAJOR fault contained.

OPTIONS

   A. The statement is not a complete sentence.
   B. The statement contains a word or phrase that is redundant.
   C. The statement contains a long, less commonly used word when a shorter, more direct word would be acceptable.
   D. The statement contains a colloquial expression that normally is avoided in business writing.

6. The fact that this activity will afford an opportunity to meet your group. 6.____

7. Do you think that the two groups can join together for next month's meeting? 7.____

8. This is one of the most exciting new innovations to be introduced into our college. 8.____

9. We expect to consummate the agenda before the meeting ends tomorrow at noon. 9.____

10. While this seminar room is small in size, we think we can use it. 10.____

11. Do you think you can make a modification in the date of the Budget Committee meeting? 11.____

12. We are cognizant of the problem but we think we can ameliorate the situation. 12.____

13. Shall I call you around three on the day I arrive in the city? 13.____

14. Until such time that we know precisely that the students will be present. 14.____

15. The consensus of opinion of all the members present is reported in the minutes. 15.____

Questions 16-25.

DIRECTIONS: For each of the sentences numbered 16 through 25, select from the options given below the MOST applicable choice.

OPTIONS

   A. The sentence is correct.
   B. The sentence contains a spelling error only.

C. The sentence contains an English grammar error only.
D. The sentence contains both a spelling error and an English grammar error.

16. Every person in the group is going to do his share. 16.____
17. The man who we selected is new to this University. 17.____
18. She is the older of the four secretaries on the two staffs that are to be combined. 18.____
19. The decision has to be made between him and I. 19.____
20. One of the volunteers are too young for this complecated task, don't you think? 20.____
21. I think your idea is splindid and it will improve this report considerably. 21.____
22. Do you think this is an exagerated account of the behavior you and me observed this morning? 22.____
23. Our supervisor has a clear idea of excelence. 23.____
24. How many occurences were verified by the observers? 24.____
25. We must complete the typing of the draft of the questionaire by noon tomorrow. 25.____
26. Which one of the following forms for the typed name of the dictator in the closing lines of a letter is *generally* MOST acceptable in the United States? 26.____

    A. (Dr.) James F. Fenton
    B. Dr. James F. Fenton
    C. Mr. James F. Fenton, Ph.D.
    D. James F. Fenton

27. Which of the following is MOST generally a rule to be followed when typing a rough draft? 27.____

    A. The copy should be single-spaced.
    B. The copy should be triple-spaced.
    C. There is no need for including footnotes.
    D. Errors must be neatly corrected.

Questions 28-30.

DIRECTIONS: Questions 28 through 30 are based on the following passage. Each paragraph within the passage contains one word that is incorrectly used because it is not in keeping with the meaning that the paragraph is evidently intended to convey. For each question, determine which word is incorrectly used and select from the choices lettered A, B, G, and D the word which, when substituted for the incorrectly used word, would BEST help to convey the meaning of the paragraph.

The office worker should avoid making errors in typing; but when errors are made, they must be unimportant. The typist should check carefully paragraph by paragraph while the memorandum, business form, report, or letter is in the typewriter. It is much easier to make corrections while the paper is in the machine. All figures, dates, and names should be checked for accuracy.

Corrections must be made on the original and on all carbon copies. If the correction is omitted only on the original and a strikeover is permitted to stand on the carbon copy, the carbon copy frequently is illegible and it is never possible to be sure after the letter has gone out that the letter itself did not contain a strikeover.

The skill of any typist may be measured by the number of errors that have been made and the way in which they have been corrected. Each error results in the loss of time and detracts from the appearance of the typed material even if it is corrected carefully. Obviously, the undesirable effects of an error are greatly reduced when the correction is made in a slovenly manner.

28. Of the following, the word which, when substituted for the incorrectly used word in the FIRST paragraph of the passage above, would BEST help to convey the meaning of the first paragraph is

    A. additions   B. corrected   C. harder   D. thoroughly

29. Of the following, the word which, when substituted for the incorrectly used word in the SECOND paragraph of the passage above, would BEST help to convey the meaning of the second paragraph is

    A. allowed   B. generally   C. made   D. remain

30. Of the following, the word which, when substituted for the incorrectly used word in the THIRD paragraph of the passage above, would BEST help to convey the meaning of the third paragraph is

    A. correction   B. increased   C. promptly   D. value

31. An office assistant needs a synonym. Of the following, the book which she would find MOST useful is

    A. a world atlas
    B. BARTLETT'S FAMILIAR QUOTATIONS
    C. a manual of style
    D. a thesaurus

32. Of the following examples of footnotes, the one that is expressed in the MOST generally accepted standard form is:
    Of the following examples of footnotes, the one that is expressed in the MOST generally accepted standard form is:

    A. Johnson, T. F. (Dr.), ENGLISH FOR EVERYONE. 3rd or 4th edition: New York City Linton Publishing Company, p. 467
    B. Frank Taylor, ENGLISH FOR TODAY (New York: Rayton Publishing Company, 1971), p. 156
    C. Ralph Wilden, ENGLISH FOR TOMORROW, Reynolds Publishing Company, England, p. 451
    D. Quinn, David, YESTERDAY'S ENGLISH (New York: Baldwin Publishing Company, 1972), p. 431

33. Standard procedures are used in offices PRIMARILY because

    A. an office is a happier place if everyone is doing the tasks in the same manner
    B. particular ways of doing jobs are considered more efficient than other ways
    C. it is good discipline for workers to follow standard procedures approved by the supervisor
    D. supervisors generally don't want workers to be creative in planning their work

34. Assume that an office assistant has the responsibility of compiling, typing and distributing a preliminary announcement of Spring course offerings. The announcement will go to approximately 900 currently enrolled students. The MOST efficient method for creating and distributing this information is to

    A. type it in MS Word and send by school e-mail
    B. type it in MS Word and send by fax
    C. send it to the graphic arts department to be published and distributed as a catalog
    D. have it posted in high-traffic areas around campus

35. "Justified typing" is a term that refers MOST specifically to copy

    A. that has been edited and for which final copy is being prepared
    B. in a form that allows for an even right-hand margin
    C. with a predetermined vertical placement for each alternate line
    D. that has been approved by the supervisor and his superior

---

KEY (CORRECT ANSWERS)

1. A	11. C	21. B	31. D
2. D	12. C	22. D	32. B
3. B	13. D	23. B	33. B
4. B	14. A	24. B	34. A
5. C	15. B	25. B	35. B
6. A	16. A	26. D	
7. B	17. C	27. B	
8. B	18. C	28. B	
9. C	19. C	29. C	
10. B	20. D	30. B	

TEST 2

DIRECTIONS: Each question or incomplete statement is followed by several suggested answers or completions. Select the one that BEST answers the question or completes the statement. *PRINT THE LETTER OF THE CORRECT ANSWER IN THE SPACE AT THE RIGHT.*

1. An office assistant was asked to mail a duplicated report of 100 pages to a professor in an out-of-town university. The professor sending the report dictated a short letter that he wanted to mail with the report.
   Of the following, the MOST inexpensive proper means of sending these two items would be to send the report

   A. and the letter first class
   B. by parcel post and the letter separately by air mail
   C. and the letter by parcel post
   D. by parcel post and attach to the package an envelope with first-class postage in which is enclosed the letter

   1.____

2. Plans are under way to determine the productivity of the typists who work in a central typewriting office.
   Of the procedures listed, the one generally considered the MOST accurate for finding out the typists' output is to

   A. keep a record of how much typing is done for specified periods of time
   B. ask each typist how fast she types when she is doing a great deal of typewriting
   C. give each typist a timed typewriting test during a specified period
   D. ask the supervisor to estimate the typing speed of each subordinate.

   2.____

3. Assume that an executive regularly receives the four types of mail listed below. As a general rule, his secretary should arrange his mail from top to bottom so that the top items are

   A. advertisements   B. printed e-mails
   C. business letters   D. unopened personal letters

   3.____

4. An office assistant in transcribing reports and letters from dictation should MOST generally assume that

   A. the transcript should be exactly what was dictated so there is little need to check any details
   B. the dictated material is merely an idea of what the dictator wanted to say so changes should be made to improve any part of the dictation
   C. there may be some slight changes, but essentially the transcription is to be a faithful copy of what was dictated
   D. the transcript is merely a very rough draft and should be typed quickly so that the dictator can review it and make changes preliminary to having the final copy typed.

   4.____

5. An office assistant in a city college is asked to place a call to a prospective visiting professor in Los Angeles. It is 1 P.M. in New York (EST). The time in Los Angeles is

   A. 9 A.M.   B. 10 A.M.   C. 4 P.M.   D. 5 P.M.

   5.____

6. An office assistant is given the task of creating a spreadsheet for faculty scheduling. The assistant should use which of the following software programs for this purpose?

    A. Microsoft Word
    B. Adobe Acrobat Pro
    C. Microsoft Excel
    D. MyFacultyScheduling iPhone app

7. An office assistant is in the process of typing the forms for recommendation for promotion for a member of the faculty who is away for a week. She notes that two books of which he is the author are listed without dates.
Of the following, the procedure she should BEST follow at this point *generally,* is to

    A. postpone doing the job until the professor returns to campus the following week
    B. type the material omitting the books
    C. check the professor's office for copies of the books and obtain the correct data
    D. call the professor's wife and ask her when the books were published.

8. An office has introduced work standards for all the employees. Of the following, it is MOST likely that use of such standards would tend to

    A. make it more difficult to determine numbers of employees needed
    B. lead to a substantial drop in morale among all of the employees
    C. reduce the possibility of planning to meet emergencies
    D. reduce uncertainty about the costs of doing tasks

9. In preparing a report that includes several tables, if not otherwise instructed, the typist should MOST properly include a list of tables

    A. in the introductory part of the report
    B. at the end of each chapter in the body of the report
    C. in the supplementary part of the report as an appendix
    D. in the supplementary part of the report as a part of the index

10. Assume that a dictator is briefly interrupted because of a telephone call or other similar matter (no more than three minutes).
Of the following tasks, the person taking the dictation should NORMALLY use the time to

    A. re-read notes already recorded
    B. tidy the dictator's desk
    C. check the accuracy of the dictator's desk files
    D. return to her own desk to type the dictated material

11. The chairman of an academic department tells an office assistant that a meeting of the faculty is to be held four weeks from the current date.
Of the following responsibilities, the office assistant is MOST frequently held responsible for

    A. planning the agenda of the meeting
    B. presiding over the conduct of the meeting
    C. reserving the meeting room and notifying the members
    D. initiating all formal resolutions.

12. For the office assistant whose duties include frequent recording and transcription of minutes of formal meetings, the one of the following reference works *generally* considered to be MOST useful is:

    A. Robert's RULES OF ORDER
    B. Bartlett's FAMILIAR QUOTATIONS
    C. WORLD ALMANAC AND BOOK OF FACTS
    D. Conway's REFERENCE

13. Of the following statements about the numeric system of filing, the one which is CORRECT is that it

    A. is the least accurate of all methods of filing
    B. eliminates the need for cross-referencing
    C. allows for very limited expansion
    D. requires a separate index

14. When more than one name or subject is involved in a piece of correspondence to be filed, the office assistant should *generally*

    A. prepare a cross-reference sheet
    B. establish a geographical filing system
    C. prepare out-guides
    D. establish a separate index card file for noting such correspondence

15. A tickler file is MOST generally used for

    A. identification of material contained in a numeric file
    B. maintenance of a current listing of telephone numbers
    C. follow-up of matters requiring future attention
    D. control of records borrowed or otherwise removed from the files

16. In filing, the name Ms. "Ann Catalana-Moss" should *generally* be indexed as

    A. Moss, Catalana, Ann (Ms.)
    B. Catalana-Moss, Ann (Ms.)
    C. Ann Catalana-Moss (Ms.)
    D. Moss-Catalana, Ann (Ms.)

17. An office assistant has a set of four cards, each of which contains one of the following names.
    In alphabetic filing, the FIRST of the cards to be filed is

    A. Ms. Alma John
    B. Mrs. John (Patricia) Edwards
    C. John-Edward School Supplies, Inc.
    D. John H. Edwards

18. Generally, of the following, the name to be filed FIRST in an alphabetical filing system is

    A. Diane Maestro   B. Diana McElroy
    C. James Mackell   D. James McKell

4 (#2)

19. According to generally recognized rules of filing in an alphabetic filing system, the one of the following names which *normally* should be filed LAST is   19._____

   A. Department of Education, New York State
   B. F. B. I.
   C. Police Department of New York City
   D. P. S. 81 of New York City

Questions 20-21.

DIRECTIONS: Answer Questions 20 and 21 SOLELY on the basis of the information provided in the following passage.

Auto: Auto travel requires prior approval by the President and/or appropriate Dean and must be indicated in the "Request for Travel Authorization" form. Employees authorised to use personal autos on official college business will be reimbursed at the rate of 14¢ per mile for the first 500 miles driven and 9¢ per mile for mileage driven in excess of 500 miles. The Comptroller's Office of the City of New York may limit the amount of reimbursement to the expenditure that would have been made if a less expensive mode of transportation (railroad, airplane, bus, etc.) had been utilized. If this occurs, the traveler will have to pick up the excess expenditure as a personal expense.

Tolls, Parking Fees and Parking Meter Fees are not reimbursable, and may NOT be claimed.

20. Suppose that Professor T. gives the office assistant the following memorandum: 20._____
    Used car for official trip to Albany, New York, and return. Distance from New York to Albany is 148 miles.
    Tolls were $1.75 each way. Parking garage cost $1.50.
    When preparing the Travel Expense Voucher for Professor T., the figure which should be claimed for transportation is

    A. $60.44   B. $56.94   C. $41.44   D. $25.72

21. Suppose that Professor V. gives the office assistant the following memorandum: 21._____
    Used car for official trip to Pittsburgh, Pennsylvania, and return. Distance from New York to Pittsburgh is 350 miles. Tolls were $1.65, $5.70 going, and $1.65, $1.00 returning.
    When preparing the Travel Expense Voucher for Professor V., the figure which should be claimed for transportation is

    A. $112.70   B. $88.00   C. $63.70   D. $49.00

Questions 22-23.

DIRECTIONS: Answer Questions 22 and 23 SOLELY on the basis of the following summary of salary increases applicable to a group of exempt student interns.

Hourly Rate - 6/30/14	Increase - 7/1/14	Increase - 7/1/15
$10.20	$1.40/hr	$1.40/hr
11.20	1.20/hr	1.20/hr
12.20	1.20/hr	1.20/hr
13.20	1.00/hr	1.00/hr
14.20	1.00/hr	1.00/hr
15.20	1.00/hr	1.00/hr

22. A college office employee with an hourly salary of $14.20 as of June 30, 2014 worked for 32 hours during the week of April 16, 2015. Her GROSS salary for that week was

   A. $422.40   B. $454.40   C. $486.40   D. $518.40

23. A college office employee was earning an hourly salary of $12.20 in June of 2014. The percentage increase in her hourly salary as of July 2, 2015 will be *most nearly* _____ percent.

   A. 10   B. 15   C. 20   D. 25

Questions 24-25.

DIRECTIONS: Answer Questions 24 and 25 SOLELY on the basis of the information contained in the following chart.

ENROLLMENT ACCORDING TO DEPARTMENTAL MAJOR

MAJOR	Borough of Manhattan Community		Bronx Community		Hostos Comm. Community		Kingsboro Community		LaGuardia Community		Bklyn. Center	N.Y.C. Community Voorhess Center	Queensboro Community	
	DAY	EVE	DAY	EVE	DAY	EVE	DAY	EVE	DAY	EVE	DAY	DAY	DAY	EVE
Accounting *	1202	4202	0802	3802			1002	4002	(1802)	(4802)	1302	1702	0902	3902
Advertising *	1273	4273												
Afro-American Studies			0837	3837							1337			
Bio-Med. Computer Sciences *														
Black Studies *											1337			
Business Administration *	1208	4208	0808	3808			1008	4008	(1808)	(4808)			0908	3908
Business Education *	1213	4213	0813	3813										
Business Management	*1273	4273							(1841)	(4841)			0941	3941
Chemical Technology *											1316			
Chemistry *			0837	3837			1039	4039			1337			
Child Care *					(1483)		1083				(1383)	1783		
Chinese														

CIRCLED SESSION CODES: THESE PROGRAMS DO NOT ADMIT NEW STUDENTS IN FEBRUARY
* COMMUNITY COLLEGE PROGRAMS WHICH ARE TRANSFERABLE TO RELATED SENIOR COLLEGE PROGRAMS

24. Suppose that a student talks with the office assistant in December about admission to a program in Business Administration as soon as possible. From the information provided in the above chart, _____ community colleges have day programs in Business Administration that begin at mid-year.

   A. Two   B. Four   C. Five   D. Six

25. Of the following majors, which one may NOT be studied during the evening at any of the community colleges shown in the above chart?

   A. Afro-American Studies
   B. Business Education
   C. Chemistry
   D. Child Care

Questions 26-27.

DIRECTIONS: Answer Questions 26 and 27 SOLELY on the basis of the information contained in the following table.

Comparison of CUNY Attrition Rates for Fall 2015 Day Freshmen through Fall 2016

Colleges	Open Admissions (a)	Regular (b)	Overall
Senior	30%	14%	21%
Community	40%	34%	39%
Total	36%	20%	29%

(a) Represents senior college students admitted with high school averages below 80 and community college students admitted with high school averages below 75.
(b) Represents senior college students admitted with averages of 80 and above and community college students admitted with averages of 75 and above.

26. The category of students who remained in the City University in the GREATEST proportion were

   A. regular students in community colleges
   B. open admissions students in community colleges
   C. regular students in senior colleges
   D. open admissions students in senior colleges

27. REGULAR admission to a senior college was on the basis of an academic average

   A. above 70
   B. of 80 or above
   C. above 75
   D. above 85

Questions 28-30.

DIRECTIONS: Answer Questions 28 through 30 SOLELY on the basis of the information contained in the passage below.

Hereafter, all SEEK students interested in transferring to community college career programs (associate degrees) from liberal arts programs in senior colleges (bachelor degrees) will be eligible for such transfers if they have completed no more than three semesters.

For students with averages of 1.5 or above, transfer will be automatic. Those with 1.0 to 1.5 averages can transfer provisionally and will be required to make substantial progress during the first semester in the career program. Once transfer has taken place, only those courses in which passing grades were received will be computed in the community college gradepoint average.

No request for transfer will be accepted from SEEK students wishing to enter the liberal arts programs at the community college.

28. According to this passage, the one of the following which is the BEST statement concerning the transfer of SEEK students is that a SEEK student

   A. may transfer to a career program at the end of one semester
   B. must complete three semester hours before he is eligible for transfer
   C. is not eligible to transfer to a career program
   D. is eligible to transfer to a liberal arts program

29. Which of the following is the BEST statement of academic evaluation for transfer purposes in the case of SEEK students?

   A. No SEEK student with an average under 1.5 may transfer.
   B. A SEEK student with an average of 1.3 may not transfer.
   C. A SEEK student with an average of 1.6 may transfer.
   D. A SEEK student with an average of .8 may transfer on a provisional basis.

30. It is MOST likely that, of the following, the NEXT degree sought by one who already holds the Associate in Science degree would be a(n)

   A. Assistantship in Science degree
   B. Associate in Applied Science degree
   C. Bachelor of Science degree
   D. Doctor of Philosophy degree

KEY (CORRECT ANSWERS)

1. D	11. C	21. B
2. A	12. A	22. C
3. D	13. D	23. C
4. C	14. A	24. B
5. B	15. C	25. D
6. C	16. B	26. C
7. C	17. D	27. B
8. D	18. C	28. A
9. A	19. B	29. C
10. A	20. C	30. C

EXAMINATION SECTION
TEST 1

DIRECTIONS: Each question or incomplete statement is followed by several suggested answers or completions. Select the one that *BEST* answers the question or completes the statement. *PRINT THE LETTER OF THE CORRECT ANSWER IN THE SPACE AT THE RIGHT.*

1. Employees tend to band together in small informal groups. Considering the effective processing of the work loads these groups *GENERALLY* should be
   A. ignored since they have no relation at all to the formal organization
   B. strongly discouraged since they result in much time wasted on personal conversations
   C. tolerated since they provide needed diversion from work pressure
   D. disbanded since they disrupt office activities

   1._____

2. It is *GENERALLY* agreed that the soundest of the following approaches to speeding up the flow of work in an office is to
   A. reduce the clerical staff by a small percentage
   B. develop a work simplification program in which employees participate in improving work methods
   C. retain major office machines beyond the suggested replacement dates
   D. have employees keep accounts of all supplies used

   2._____

3. Of the following, the one which usually *BEST* encourages group cohesiveness is
   A. setting up an opportunity for competition among the members
   B. creating opportunities for group members to communicate with each other
   C. increasing the size of the group
   D. pointing out to the group the most effective members of the group in each office

   3._____

4. Suppose that a student arrives for an appointment with a professor while you, the professor's secretary, are typing an important memo. Of the following, it would normally be *BEST* for you to
   A. explain that you have a very important memo to type and request that the student have a seat
   B. finish typing the memo before acknowledging the student's presence
   C. point out the professor's office and tell the student to go right in
   D. stop typing, check to be sure the professor is free, and then escort the student into the professor's office

   4._____

5. Upward communications in an organization are MOST generally facilitated when
   A. messages are carefully screened by the first-line supervisors
   B. there is a clear line of movement of messages upward so that messages flow quickly and everyone understands the movement
   C. there is a lack of acceptance of criticism from subordinates
   D. the types of messages that are acceptable are specified exactly

   5._____

6. Suppose that a student enters your office and asks to see a Professor Carlson. The student is in the wrong office and you do not know where Professor Carlson is located. Of the following, it would *generally* be BEST for you to
   A. ask the student to wait while you check the office directory
   B. direct the student to an information desk on another floor
   C. politely inform the student that you do not know where Professor Carlson is located and therefore cannot offer assistance
   D. suggest that the student try the office next door

7. Suppose that another office assistant tells you: "I would never take anything of great value from the office, but who is going to miss a few pencils and scotch tape? I take these things regularly." Of the following, the BEST way for you to react to this statement *generally* should be to
   A. agree with the office assistant and tell her that these small items don't add up to much in the huge budget of the college
   B. comment to the office assistant that she shouldn't worry at all about taking items because others are doing the same thing and it is just accepted
   C. comment to the office assistant that the principle of honesty applies irrespective of the dollar value of the items taken
   D. refrain from making any comment since nothing would be gained by further discussion on such a topic

8. A certain office assistant has a poor tardiness record and was recently warned by her supervisor that certain disciplinary action would be taken if she were late again. If she comes in late again, in private, the supervisor SHOULD
   A. speak to her right away and, after listening to her explanation, impose any warranted discipline quietly and impersonally
   B. speak to her during the next afternoon this will prevent an emotional confrontation and will give her time to fully realize the consequences of her actions
   C. speak to her right away and make an attempt to soften the necessary disciplinary action by apologizing for having to use discipline
   D. speak to her right away, and remind her in no uncertain terms of the difficulty she has caused him by her continual lateness before imposing any warranted discipline

9. Suppose that you are a secretary to a professor who has been called to an emergency conference fifteen minutes before a scheduled appointment with a student. When the student arrives, you normally should apologize for the inconvenience *and,* if no appointment with him is available the same day,
   A. arrange for another professor to see the student if the matter is one which can be handled by someone else
   B. make a tentative appointment for a later date even if you do not know the professor's schedule
   C. request that the student call for another appointment
   D. request that the student wait even if it is unknown how long the professor will be away

10. Of the following, it is *generally* agreed that the *BEST* way to get feedback as to whether information communicated has been understood is to ask the person who has received the information
    A. whether information just communicated was understood
    B. whether there are any questions about the information just communicated
    C. questions about the information that require yes or no answers
    D. questions that require use of the information in answering

11. One aspect of stereotyping and evaluating the source is the tendency to ignore the "grays" and to react in "black or white" terms. Thus, when someone is speaking who has gained our trust or who begins a speech by saying something with which we agree, we will hear nearly everything he says as good and correct. On the other hand, someone we distrust will be ignored or heard to say nothing worth attending to.

    This failure to discriminate between the "good" and "bad" that may be intermixed within a single person and his comments is *MOST* appropriately referred to as
    A. the negative feedback   B. bureaucracy
    C. the halo effect   D. Parkinson's law

12. A supervisory approach in which each phase of the job is specified in detail, supervision is close, and people are allowed little discretion in performing their jobs, *MOST GENERALLY*
    A. is preferred by most subordinates and provides motivation to work harder
    B. provides little or no incentive to work harder than the minimum required
    C. creates undue pressure which usually results in increased performance
    D. works better in the long run than in the short run

13. Those who have studied the phenomenon of the office "grapevine" *MOST GENERALLY* have found that
    A. the truth is always conveyed via the "grapevine"
    B. the "grapevine" often performs a useful service by correcting some of the shortcomings of the formal communication system
    C. the "grapevine" naturally interferes with the satisfactory functioning of the formal communication system which has been established
    D. efforts to destroy the "grapevine" are successful

14. It is *generally* agreed that on-the-job training is *MOST* effective when new employees are
    A. allowed to watch highly skilled employees perform the job and subsequently follow the same procedures on their own
    B. shown the job operations step by step and allowed to practice under close supervision
    C. provided with procedures manuals that outline the job operations in clear, easy-to-understand language, instead of receiving personal instructions
    D. put to work immediately for motivational purposes and then learn job routines principally by trial and error

15. The supervisor criticizes an office assistant who, although a good worker, is consistently late in the morning, although she lives just a short subway ride away from the office. She is also late after lunch. The MOST desirable reaction for the office assistant in such a situation is to
    A. realize that many of her friends are also late but they have nicer supervisors so there is really no need to note what the supervisor said to her
    B. keep track of others who are late and remind the supervisor that others are also late
    C. realize that she should be prompt and make adjustments in her activities so that in the future she does get to work on time
    D. realize that she is one of the better workers and is able to accomplish as much in an hour as the average worker accomplishes in two hours

16. When a supervisor finds it necessary to let a subordinate know that he is dissatisfied with the subordinate's level of performance, which of the following tactics would usually prove MOST effective in improving the subordinate's performance?
    A. The supervisor should be angry when criticizing in order to prevent the mistakes from recurring.
    B. Once criticism has been made, the supervisor should be sure to continuously impress the seriousness of the mistakes upon the subordinate.
    C. When making his criticism, the supervisor should guard against referring to any work that was well done. since this would reduce the effect of his criticism.
    D. The supervisor should focus his criticism on the mistakes being made and should avoid downgrading the subordinate personally.

17. Of the following, the BEST descriptive statement of an effective supervisor is *generally,* that he
    A. works alongside his subordinates on the same type of work
    B. catches all errors when they are made
    C. gives many specific work orders and few general work orders
    D. devotes much of his time to long-range activities, such as planning and improving human relations

18. When a new method of performing a job operation is to be instituted, the one of the following approaches which will MOST generally gain acceptance of the change by subordinates is to
    A. hold a friendly, informal meeting after the change has been implemented to explain the advantages of the new method
    B. consult the subordinates involved in the change as early as possible in the planning stage
    C. work closely with just one of the subordinates who will be affected by the change so that others need not be taken off the job
    D. implement the change, instruct employees fully in the new method, and then follow up on results

19. Of the following, a supervisor interested in setting quality standards for work produced by his subordinates PRIMARILY should
    A. consult with office supervisors in other organizations to determine the range of acceptable standards
    B. institute a quality improvement program and set standards at the point where quality levels off at desirable levels
    C. establish an ad hoc committee comprised of a representative sample of office workers to set firm and exacting standards
    D. consult the Quality Standards Handbook which predetermines with mathematical precision the level that office quality should meet

19._____

20. During a conversation with his supervisor, a subordinate begins to discuss what appears to the supervisor to be a deep-seated personality problem that has been bothering the subordinate. For the supervisor to suggest to the subordinate the possibility of professional help would NORMALLY be
    A. *undesirable;* the necessity of requiring professional help would automatically disqualify the subordinate from being promoted in the future
    B. *desirable;* generally a supervisor can be of limited assistance in personally solving deep-seated personality problems
    C. *undesirable;* since the supervisor was approached by the employee it is his responsibility as a supervisor to help the employee solve his problem
    D. *desirable;* in accordance with the Civil Service Commission regulations a supervisor is not allowed to get involved in subordinates personal problems

20._____

21. Of the followings, the supervisory practice which is LEAST likely to produce a favorable work environment is that the supervisor
    A. takes an active interest in subordinates
    B. does not tolerate mistakes regardless of who has made the mistake
    C. gives praise when justified
    D. disciplines individuals in accordance with their violation of the rules

21._____

22. Choosing supervisors strictly from within a particular working section GENERALLY is
    A. *desirable,* primarily because the budgeting necessary for promotion is substantially decreased
    B. *undesirable* because personal preferences will always outweigh merit
    C. *desirable* primarily because a good worker within that section will be a good supervisor for that section alone
    D. *undesirable,* primarily because the pool of candidates will be severely limited

22._____

23. The chairman of an academic department is currently in conference and has appointments scheduled for the remainder of the day. He has requested that the office assistant keep interruptions to a minimum. A caller, who does not have an appointment and who refuses to identify himself other than to say that he is a student insists upon seeing the chairman. Of the following, the MOST appropriate action to be taken by the office assistant *generally* would be to
    A. courteously but firmly refuse admittance, and offer to schedule an appointment for another day
    B. tell the student that he may wait and will probably be able to see the chairman between other scheduled appointments
    C. ask the student to wait while she consults with the chairman to determine if this is a legitimate interruption
    D. send the student in to the chairman's office to ask if he may interrupt the chairman briefly

23.____

24. An office assistant who has been out of her office for an hour returns and notices a visitor whose presence has apparently not been acknowledged by any of the other office workers. Of the following, the MOST appropriate action for her to take is to
    A. request the office worker seated closest to the front to assist the visitor
    B. return to her desk and wait for one of the other office workers to recognize the visitor's presence
    C. walk to the middle of the office and announce, "There's a visitor present."
    D. offer assistance to the visitor immediately.

24.____

25. Assume that Dr. Jones, the coordinator of the teacher education program is in Washington to present a proposal for funding of a research project. During his absence, a Professor Van Slyke, who identifies himself as a professor from another university, telephones and asks to speak with Dr. Jones. Of the following, the MOST appropriate reply for the college office assistant to make is:
    A. "He is in Washington, D.C. Please try again tomorrow."
    B. "He is not in the office today he will be back tomorrow morning. May I ask him to call you then?"
    C. He's on an interview down at the U.S. Office of Education. Is there anything I might do to assist you ?"
    D. "Please try again tomorrow. Dr. Jones is out seeking funds for our education research program."

25.____

KEY (CORRECT ANSWERS)

1. C
2. B
3. B
4. D
5. B

6. A
7. C
8. A
9. A
10. D

11. C
12. B
13. B
14. B
15. C

16. D
17. D
18. B
19. B
20. B

21. B
22. D
23. A
24. D
25. B

EXAMINATION SECTION
TEST 1

DIRECTIONS: Each question or incomplete statement is followed by several suggested answers or completions. Select the one that BEST answers the question or completes the statement. *PRINT THE LETTER OF THE CORRECT ANSWER IN THE SPACE AT THE RIGHT.*

1. A matriculated student at the City University of New York may BEST be described as one who
   A. is allowed a maximum credit load of 12 credits
   B. has paid full tuition
   C. has been admitted to the City University conditionally
   D. is enrolled in a program leading to a degree

   1.____

2. The Administrative Council of the City University of New York consists of the _____ of the University colleges.
   A. presidents
   B. vice presidents
   C. directors of divisions
   D. deans of administration

   2.____

3. Of the following, the statement which BEST describes the policy of open admissions at the City University of New York is that
   A. any resident of New York City may visit and participate at any time in any classes offered by the City University
   B. all recent graduates of New York City high schools are eligible for admission to a college of the City University
   C. any adult is eligible for admission to the City University regardless of his educational background
   D. minority group members are assured of admission regardless of educational background

   3.____

4. Of the following degrees, the one which the community colleges of the City University of New York GENERALLY have the authority to grant is the _____ degree.
   A. master's   B. bachelor's   C. specialist's   D. associate's

   4.____

5. Normally, a prospective student who is the holder of a New York State high school equivalency diploma
   A. is generally eligible for admission to undergraduate units of the City University
   B. will need to present a high school certificate as well as the equivalency diploma for admission to the City University
   C. is eligible for admission only to non-transfer programs of the community college units
   D. will need to qualify for admission by enrolling in an evening division program as a special student

   5.____

6. The FIRST terminal degree given by graduate schools normally is a _____ degree.
   A. doctor's   B. associates   C. specialist's   D. master's

7. Generally, non-matriculated students at the City University of New York would MOST frequently be enrolled in
   A. evening sessions
   B. day sessions
   C. a graduate division
   D. a liberal arts college

8. The City University of New York is an educational institution consisting of
   A. all public and private colleges located in New York City
   B. only the community colleges located in the five boroughs of New York City
   C. the municipal college system of New York City
   D. the graduate and professional schools financed in part by the City of New York

9. An employment officer seeking to recruit prospective medical laboratory technicians from the City University of New York should recruit PRIMARILY in
   A. schools of education
   B. university doctoral programs
   C. community colleges
   D. liberal arts programs

10. The CHIEF educational and administrative officer of the City University of New York as a whole is called the
    A. Chancellor
    B. President
    C. Vice Chairman of the Board
    D. University Dean

KEY (CORRECT ANSWERS)

1.	D	6.	D
2.	A	7.	A
3.	B	8.	C
4.	D	9.	C
5.	A	10.	A

EXAMINATION SECTION
TEST 1

DIRECTIONS: Each question or incomplete statement is followed by several suggested answers or completions. Select the one that BEST answers the question or completes the statement. *PRINT THE LETTER OF THE CORRECT ANSWER IN THE SPACE AT THE RIGHT.*

Questions 1-5.

DIRECTIONS: Questions 1 through 5 consist of a sentence with an underlined word. For each question, select the choice that is CLOSEST in meaning to the underlined word.

EXAMPLE
This division reviews the fiscal reports of the agency.
In this sentence, the word *fiscal* means MOST NEARLY
    A. financial   B. critical   C. basic   D. personnel
The correct answer is A. "financial" because "financial" is closest to *fiscal*. Therefore, the answer is A.

1. Every good office worker needs basic skills.
   The word *basic* in this sentence means
      A. fundamental   B. advanced   C. unusual   D. outstanding

2. He turned out to be a good instructor.
   The word *instructor* in this sentence means
      A. student   B. worker   C. typist   D. teacher

3. The quantity of work in the office was under study.
   In this sentence, the word *quantity* means
      A. amount   B. flow   C. supervision   D. type

4. The morning was spent examining the time records.
   In this sentence, the word *examining* means
      A. distributing   B. collecting   C. checking   D. filing

5. The candidate filled in the proper spaces on the form.
   In this sentence, the word *proper* means
      A. blank   B. appropriate   C. many   D. remaining

Questions 6-8.

DIRECTIONS: Questions 6 through 8 are to be answered SOLELY on the basis of the information contained in the following paragraph.

The increase in the number of public documents in the last two centuries closely matches the increase in population in the United States. The great number of public documents has become a serious threat to their usefulness. It is necessary to have programs which will reduce the number of public documents that are kept and which will, at the same time, assure keeping those that have value. Such programs need a great deal of thought to have any success.

6. According to the above paragraph, public documents may be less useful if　　　　6.____
    A. the files are open to the public
    B. the record room is too small
    C. the copying machine is operated only during normal working hours
    D. too many records are being kept

7. According to the above paragraph, the growth of the population in the United　　　　7.____
States has matched the growth in the quantity of public documents for a period of MOST NEARLY _____ years.
    A. 50   B. 100   C. 200   D. 300

8. According to the above paragraph, the increased number of public documents　　　　8.____
has made it necessary to
    A. find out which public documents are worth keeping
    B. reduce the great number of public documents by decreasing government services
    C. eliminate the copying of all original public documents
    D. avoid all new copying devices

Questions 9-10.

DIRECTIONS: Questions 9 and 10 are to be answered SOLELY on the basis of the information contained in the following paragraph.

The work goals of an agency can best be reached if the employees understand and agree with these goals. One way to gain such understanding and agreement is for management to encourage and seriously consider suggestions from employees in the setting of agency goals.

9. On the basis of the above paragraph, the BEST way to achieve the work goals　　　　9.____
of an agency is to
    A. make certain that employees work as hard as possible
    B. study the organizational structure of the agency
    C. encourage employees to think seriously about the agency's problems
    D. stimulate employee understanding of the work goals

10. On the basis of the above paragraph, understanding and agreement with agency goals can be gained by 10._____
    A. allowing the employees to set agency goals
    B. reaching agency goals quickly
    C. legislative review of agency operations
    D. employee participation in setting agency goals

Questions 11-15.

DIRECTIONS: Each of Questions 11 through 15 consists of a group of four words. One word in each group is incorrectly spelled. For each question, print the letter of the correct answer in the space at the right that is the same as the letter next to the word which is INCORRECTLY spelled.

EXAMPLE

A. housing   B. certain   C. budgit   D. money

The word "budgit" is incorrectly spelled, because the correct spelling should be "budget." Therefore, the correct answer is C.

11. A. sentince   B. bulletin   C. notice   D. definition   11._____
12. A. appointment   B. exactly   C. typest   D. light   12._____
13. A. penalty   B. suparvise   C. consider   D. division   13._____
14. A. schedule   B. accurate   C. corect   D. simple   14._____
15. A. suggestion   B. installed   C. proper   D. agincy   15._____

Questions 16-20.

DIRECTIONS: Each Question 16 through 20 consists of a sentence which may be
    A. incorrect because of bad word usage, or
    B. incorrect because of bad punctuation, or
    C. incorrect because of bad spelling, or
    D. correct
    Read each sentence carefully. Then print in the space at the right A, B, C, or D, according to the answer you choose from the four choices listed above. There is only one type of error in each incorrect sentence. If there is no error, the sentence is correct.

EXAMPLE

George Washington was the father of his contry.
This sentence is incorrect because of bad spelling ("contry" instead of "country").
Therefore, the answer is C.

16. The assignment was completed in record time but the payroll for it has not yet been preparid. 16._____

17. The operator, on the other hand, is willing to learn me how to use the mimeograph. 17._____

18. She is the prettiest of the three sisters. 18._____

19. She doesn't know; if the mail has arrived. 19._____

20. The doorknob of the office door is broke. 20._____

21. A clerk can process a form in 15 minutes.
    How many forms can that clerk process in six hours?
    A. 10   B. 21   C. 24   D. 90   21._____

22. An office staff consists of 120 people. Sixty of them have been assigned to a special project. Of the remaining staff, 20 answer the mail, 10 handle phone calls, and the rest operate the office machines.
    The number of people operating the office machines is
    A. 20   B. 30   C. 40   D. 45   22._____

23. An office worker received 65 applications but on the first day had to return 26 of them for being incomplete and on the second day 25 had to be returned for being incomplete.
    How many applications did NOT have to be returned?
    A. 10   B. 12   C. 14   D. 16   23._____

24. An office worker answered 63 phone calls in one day and 91 phone calls the next day.
    For these 2 days, what was the average number of phone calls he answered per day?
    A. 77   B. 28   C. 82   D. 93   24._____

25. An office worker processed 12 vouchers of $8.50 each, 3 vouchers of $3.68 each, and 2 vouchers of $1.29 each.
    The TOTAL dollar amount of these vouchers is
    A. $116.04   B. $117.52   C. $118.62   D. $119.04   25._____

KEY (CORRECT ANSWERS)

1.	A		11.	A
2.	D		12.	C
3.	A		13.	B
4.	C		14.	C
5.	B		15.	D
6.	D		16.	C
7.	C		17.	A
8.	A		18.	D
9.	D		19.	B
10.	D		20.	A

21. C
22. B
23. C
24. A
25. C

TEST 2

DIRECTIONS: Each question or incomplete statement is followed by several suggested answers or completions. Select the one that BEST answers the question or completes the statement. *PRINT THE LETTER OF THE CORRECT ANSWER IN THE SPACE AT THE RIGHT.*

Questions 1-5.

DIRECTIONS: Each Question from 1 through 5 lists four names. The names may not be exactly the same. Compare the names in each question and mark your answer
- A if all the names are different
- B if only two names are exactly the same
- C if only three names are exactly the same
- D if all four names are exactly the same

EXAMPLE
Jensen, Alfred E.
Jensen, Alfred E.
Jensan, Alfred E.
Jensen, Fred E.

Since the name Jensen, Alfred E. appears twice and is exactly the same in both places, the correct answer is B.

1. A. Riviera, Pedro S.   B. Rivers, Pedro S.
   C. Riviera, Pedro N.   D. Riviera, Juan S.

2. A. Guider, Albert   B. Guidar, Albert
   C. Giuder, Alfred   D. Guider, Albert

3. A. Blum, Rona   B. Blum, Rona
   C. Blum, Rona   D. Blum, Rona

4. A. Raugh, John   B. Raugh, James
   C. Raughe, John   D. Raugh, John

5. A. Katz, Stanley   B. Katz, Stanley
   C. Katze, Stanley   D. Katz, Stanley

Questions 6-10.

DIRECTIONS: Each Question 6 through 10 consists of numbers or letters in Columns I and II. For each question, compare each line of Column I with its corresponding line in Column II and decide how many lines in Column I are EXACTLY the same as their corresponding lines in Column II. In your answer space, mark your answer
- A if only ONE line in Column I is exactly the same as its corresponding line in Column II
- B if only TWO lines in Column I are exactly the same as their corresponding lines in Column II

2 (#2)

C if only THREE lines in Column I are exactly the same as their corresponding lines in Column II
D if all FOUR lines in Column I are exactly the same as their corresponding lines in Column II

EXAMPLE

Column I	Column II
1776	1776
1865	1865
1945	1945
1976	1978

Only three lines in Column I are exactly the same as their corresponding lines in Column II. Therefore, the correct answer is C.

	Column I	Column II	
6.	5653 8727 ZPSS 4952	5653 8728 ZPSS 9453	6.____
7.	PNJP NJPJ JNPN PNJP	PNPJ NJPJ JNPN PNPJ	7.____
8.	effe uWvw KpGj vmnv	eFfe uWvw KpGg vmnv	8.____
9.	5232 PfrC zssz rwwr	5232 PfrN zzss rwww	9.____
10.	czws cecc thrm lwtz	czws cece thrm lwtz	10.____

Questions 11-15.

DIRECTIONS: Questions 11 through 15 have lines of letters and numbers. Each letter should be matched with its number in accordance with the following table.

Letter	F	R	C	A	W	L	E	N	B	T
Matching Number	0	1	2	3	4	5	6	7	8	9

From the table you can determine that the letter F has the matching number 0 below it, the letter R has the matching number 1 below, etc.

For each question, compare each line of letters and numbers carefully to see if each letter has its correct matching number. If all the letters and numbers are matched correctly in

none of the lines of the question, mark your answer A
only *one* of the lines of the question, mark your answer B
only *two* of the lines of the question, mark your answer C
all three lines of the question, mark your answer D

EXAMPLE

WBCR	4826
TLBF	9580
ATNE	3986

There is a mistake in the first line because the letter R should have its matching number 1 instead of the number 6.

The second line is correct because each letter shown has the correct matching number.

There is a mistake in the third line because the letter N should have the matching number 7 instead of the number 8.

Since all the letters and numbers are correct matched in only one of the lines in the sample, the correct answer is B.

11. EBCT   6829
    ATWR   3961
    NLBW   7584

12. RNCT   1729
    LNCR   5728
    WAEB   5368

13. NTWB   7948
    RABL   1385
    TAEF   9360

14. LWRB   5417
    RLWN   1647
    CBWA   2843

15. ABTC   3792
    WCER   5261
    AWCN   3417

16. Your job often brings you into contact with the public.
    Of the following, it would be MOST desirable to explain the reasons for official actions to people coming into your office for assistance because such explanations
    A. help build greater understanding between the public and your agency
    B. help build greater self-confidence in city employees
    C. convince the public that nothing they do can upset a city employee
    D. show the public that city employees are intelligent

17. Assume that you strongly dislike one of your co-workers.
You should FIRST
    A. discuss your feeling with the co-worker
    B. demand a transfer to another office
    C. suggest to your supervisor that the co-worker should be observed carefully
    D. try to figure out the reason for this dislike before you say or do anything

18. An office worker who has problems accepting authority is MOST likely to find it difficult to
    A. obey rules
    B. understand people
    C. assist other employees
    D. follow complex instructions

19. The employees in your office have taken a dislike to one person and frequently annoy her.
Your supervisor should
    A. transfer this person to another unit at the first opportunity
    B. try to find out the reason for the staff's attitude before doing anything about it
    C. threaten to transfer the first person observed bothering this person
    D. ignore the situation

20. Assume that your supervisor has asked a worker in your office to get a copy of a report out of the files. You notice the worker as accidentally pulled out the wrong report.
Of the following, the BEST way for you to handle this situation is to tell
    A. the worker about all the difficulties that will result from this error
    B. the worker about her mistake in a nice way
    C. the worker to ignore this error
    D. your supervisor that this worker needs more training in how to use the files

21. Filing systems differ in their efficiency.
Which of the following is the BEST way to evaluate the efficiency of a filing system? A
    A. number of times used per day
    B. amount of material that is received each day for filing
    C. amount of time it takes to locate material
    D. type of locking system used

22. In planning ahead so that a sufficient amount of general office supplies is always available, it would be LEAST important to find out the
    A. current office supply needs of the staff
    B. amount of office supplies used last year
    C. days and times that office supplies can be ordered
    D. agency goals and objectives

23. The MAIN reason for establishing routine office work procedures is that once a routine is established
    A. work need not be checked for accuracy
    B. all steps in the routine will take an equal amount of time to perform
    C. each time the job is repeated, it will take less time to perform
    D. each step in the routine will not have to be planned all over again each time

24. When an office machine centrally located in an agency must be shut down for repairs, the bureaus and divisions using this machine should be informed of the
    A. expected length of time before the machine will be in operation again
    B. estimated cost of repairs
    C. efforts being made to avoid future repairs
    D. type of new equipment which the agency may buy in the future to replace the machine being repaired

25. If the day's work is properly scheduled, the MOST important result would be that the
    A. supervisor will not have to do much supervision
    B. employee will know what to do next
    C. employee will show greater initiative
    D. job will become routine

KEY (CORRECT ANSWERS)

1.	A		11.	C
2.	B		12.	B
3.	D		13.	D
4.	B		14.	B
5.	C		15.	A
6.	B		16.	A
7.	B		17.	D
8.	B		18.	A
9.	A		19.	B
10.	C		20.	B

21. C
22. D
23. D
24. A
25. B

EXAMINATION SECTION
TEST 1

DIRECTIONS: Each question or incomplete statement is followed by several suggested answers or completions. Select the one that BEST answers the question or completes the statement. *PRINT THE LETTER OF THE CORRECT ANSWER IN THE SPACE AT THE RIGHT.*

1. Assume that a few co-workers meet near your desk and talk about personal matters during working hours. Lately, this practice has interfered with your work.
   In order to stop this practice, the BEST action for you to take FIRST is to
   A. ask your supervisor to put a stop to the co-workers' meeting near your desk
   B. discontinue any friendship with this group
   C. ask your co-workers not to meet near your desk
   D. request that your desk be moved to another location

   1.____

2. In order to maintain office coverage during working hours, your supervisor has scheduled your lunch hour from 1 P.M. to 2 P.M. and your co-workers' lunch hour from 12 P.M. to 1 P.M. Lately, your co-worker has been returning late from lunch each day. As a result, you don't get a full hour since you must return to the office by 2 P.M.
   Of the following, the BEST action for you to take FIRST is to
   A. explain to your co-worker in a courteous manner that his lateness is interfering with your right to a full hour for lunch
   B. tell your co-worker that his lateness must stop or you will report him to your supervisor
   C. report your co-worker's lateness to your supervisor
   D. leave at 1 P.M. for lunch, whether your co-worker has returned or not

   2.____

3. Assume that, as an office worker, one of your jobs is to open mail sent to your unit, read the mail for content, and send the mail to the appropriate person to handle. You accidentally open and begin to read a letter marked *personal* to a co-worker.
   Of the following, the BEST action for you to take is to
   A. report to your supervisor that your co-worker is receiving personal mail at the office
   B. destroy the letter so that your co-worker does not know you saw it
   C. reseal the letter and place it on the co-worker's desk without saying anything
   D. bring the letter to your co-worker and explain that you opened it by accident

   3.____

4. Suppose that in evaluating your work, your supervisor gives you an overall rating, but states that you sometimes turn in work with careless errors.
The BEST action for you to take would be to
   A. ask a co-worker who is good at details to proofread your work
   B. take time to do a careful job, paying more attention to detail
   C. continue working as usual since occasional errors are to be expected
   D. ask your supervisor if she would mind correcting your errors

4._____

5. Assume that you are taking a telephone message for a co-worker who is not in the office at the time.
Of the following, the LEAST important item to write on the message is the
   A. length of the call   B. name of the caller
   C. time of the call   D. telephone number of the caller

5._____

Questions 6-13.

DIRECTIONS: Questions 6 through 13 each consist of a sentence which may or may not be an example of good English. The underlined parts of each sentence may be correct or incorrect. Examine each sentence, considering grammar, punctuation, spelling, and capitalization. If the English usage in the underlined parts of the sentence given is better than any of the changes in the underlined words suggested in Options B, C, or D, choose Option A. If the changes in the underlined words suggested in Options B, C, or D would make the sentence correct, choose the correct option. Do not choose an option that will change the meaning of the sentence.

6. This Fall, the office will be closed on Columbus Day, October 9th.
   A. Correct as is   B. fall...Columbus Day, October
   C. Fall...Columbus day, October   D. fall...Columbus Day, october

6._____

7. This manual discribes the duties performed by an Office Aide.
   A. Correct as is   B. describe the duties performed
   C. discribe the duties performed   D. describes the duties performed

7._____

8. There weren't no paper in the supply closet.
   A. Correct as is   B. weren't any
   C. wasn't any   D. wasn't no

8._____

9. The new employees left there office to attend a meeting.
   A. Correct as is   B. they're
   C. their   D. thier

9._____

10. The office worker started working at 8:30 a.m.
    A. Correct as is   B. 8:30 a.m.
    C. 8;30 a,m.   D. 8:30 am.

10._____

11. The alphabet, or A to Z sequence are the basis of most filing systems.
    A. Correct as is   B. alphabet, or A to Z sequence, is
    C. alphabet, or A to Z sequence are   D. alphabet, or A too Z sequence, is

11._____

12. <u>Those</u> file cabinets are five <u>feet</u> tall. 12.____
    A. Correct as is B. Them...feet
    C. Those...foot D. Them...foot

13. The Office Aide checked the <u>register and finding</u> the date of the meeting. 13.____
    A. Correct as is B. regaster and finding
    C. register and found D. regaster and found

Questions 14-21.

DIRECTIONS: Each of Questions 14 through 21 has two lists of numbers. Each list contains three sets of numbers. Check each of the three sets in the list on the right to see if they are the same as the corresponding set in the list on the left. Mark your answers
    A. if none of the sets in the right list are the same as those in the left list
    B. if only one of the sets in the right list are the same as those in the left list
    C. if only two of the sets in the right list are the same as those in the left list
    D. if all three sets in the right list are the same as those in the left list

14. 7354183476   7354983476 14.____
    4474747744   4474747774
    57914302311   57914302311

15. 7143592185   7143892185 15.____
    8344517699   8344518699
    9178531263   9178531263

16. 2572114731   257214731 16.____
    8806835476   8806835476
    8255831246   8255831246

17. 331476853821   331476858621 17.____
    6976658532996   6976655832996
    3766042113715   3766042113745

18. 8806663315   8806663315 18.____
    74477138449   74477138449
    211756663666   211756663666

19. 990006966996   99000696996 19.____
    53022219743   53022219843
    4171171117717   4171171177717

20. 24400222433004   24400222433004 20.____
    5300030055000355   5300030055500355
    20000075532002022   20000075532002022

21. 6111666406600011116   61116664066001116   21._____
     7111300117001100733   7111300117001100733
     26666446664476518   26666446664476518

Questions 22-25.

DIRECTIONS: Each of Questions 22 through 25 has two lists of names and addresses. Each list contains three sets of names and addresses. Check each of the three sets in the list on the right to see if they are the same as the corresponding set in the list on the left. Mark your answers
    A. if none of the sets in the right list are the same as those in the left list
    B. if only one of the sets in the right list are the same as those in the left list
    C. if only two of the sets in the right list are the same as those in the left list
    D. if all three sets in the right list are the same as those in the left list

22.   Mary T. Berlinger   Mary T. Berlinger   22._____
      2351 Hampton St.   2351 Hampton St.
      Monsey, N.Y. 20117   Monsey, N.Y. 20117

      Eduardo Benes   Eduardo Benes
      473 Kingston Avenue   473 Kingston Avenue
      Central Islip, N.Y. 11734   Central Islip, N.Y. 11734

      Alan Carrington Fuchs   Alan Carrington Fuchs
      17 Gnarled Hollow Road   17 Gnarled Hollow Road
      Los Angeles, CA 91635   Los Angeles, CA 91685

23.   David John Jacobson   David John Jacobson   23._____
      178 35 St. Apt. 4C   178 53 St. Apt. 4C
      New York, N.Y. 00927   New York, N.Y. 00927

      Ann-Marie Calonella   Ann-Marie Calonella
      7243 South Ridge Blvd.   7243 South Ridge Blvd.
      Bakersfield, CA 96714   Bakersfield, CA 96714

      Pauline M. Thompson   Pauline M. Thomson
      872 Linden Ave.   872 Linden Ave.
      Houston, Texas 70321   Houston, Texas 70321

24.   Chester LeRoy Masterton   Chester LeRoy Masterson   24._____
      152 Lacy Rd.   152 Lacy Rd.
      Kankakee, Ill. 54532   Kankakee, Ill. 54532

      William Maloney   William Maloney
      S. LaCrosse Pla.   S. LaCross Pla.
      Wausau, Wisconsin 52146   Wausau, Wisconsin 52146

5 (#1)

Cynthia V. Barnes
16 Pines Rd.
Greenpoint, Miss. 20376

Cynthia V. Barnes
16 Pines Rd.
Greenpoint, Miss. 20376

25. Marcel Jean Frontenac
6 Burton On The Water
Calender, Me. 01471

Marcel Jean Frontenac
6 Burton On The Water
Calender, Me. 01471

25.____

J. Scott Marsden
174 S. Tipton St.
Cleveland, Ohio

J. Scott Marsden
174 Tipton St.
Cleveland, Ohio

Lawrence T. Haney
171 McDonough St.
Decatur, Ga. 31304

Lawrence T. Haney
171 McDonough St.
Decatur, Ga. 31304

KEY (CORRECT ANSWERS)

1.	C		11.	B
2.	A		12.	A
3.	D		13.	C
4.	B		14.	B
5.	A		15.	B
6.	B		16.	C
7.	D		17.	A
8.	C		18.	D
9.	C		19.	A
10.	B		20.	C

21. C
22. C
23. B
24. B
25. C

TEST 2

DIRECTIONS: Each question or incomplete statement is followed by several suggested answers or completions. Select the one that BEST answers the question or completes the statement. *PRINT THE LETTER OF THE CORRECT ANSWER IN THE SPACE AT THE RIGHT.*

Questions 1-6.

DIRECTIONS: Questions 1 through 6 are to be answered SOLELY on the basis of the information contained in the following passage.

Duplicating is the process of making a number of identical copies of letters, document, etc. from an original. Some duplicating processes make copies directly from the original document. Other duplicating processes require the preparation of a special master, and copies are then made from the master. Four of the most common duplicating processes are stencil, fluid, offset, and xerox.

In the stencil process, the typewriter is used to cut the words into a master called a stencil. Drawings, charts, or graphs can be cut into the stencil using a stylus. As many as 3,500 good-quality copies can be reproduced from one stencil. Various grades of finished paper from inexpensive mimeograph to expensive bond can be used.

The fluid process is a good method of copying from 50 to 125 good-quality copies from a master, which is prepared with a special dye. The master is placed on the duplicator, and special paper with a hard finish is moistened and then passed through the duplicator. Some of the dye on the master is dissolved, creating an impression on the paper. The impression becomes lighter as more copies are made; and once the dye on the master is used up, a new master must be made.

The offset process is the most adaptable office duplicating process because this process can be used for making a few copies or many copies. Masters can be made on paper or plastic for a few hundred copies, or on metal plates for as many as 75,000 copies. By using a special technique called photo-offset, charts, photographs, illustrations, or graphs can be reproduced on the master plate. The offset process is capable of producing large quantities of fine, top-quality copies on all types of finished paper.

The xerox process reproduces an exact duplicate from an original. It is the fastest duplicating method because the original material is placed directly on the duplicator, eliminating the need to make a special master. Any kind of paper can be used. The xerox process is the most expensive duplicating process; however, it is the best method of reproducing small quantities of good-quality copies of reports, letters, official documents, memos, or contracts.

1. Of the following, the MOST efficient method of reproducing 5,000 copies of a graph is
   A. stencil   B. fluid   C. offset   D. xerox

1._____

2. The offset process is the MOST adaptable office duplicating process because
   A. it is the quickest duplicating method
   B. it is the least expensive duplicating method
   C. it can produce a small number or large number of copies
   D. a softer master can be used over and over again

3. Which one of the following duplicating processes uses moistened paper?
   A. Stencil B. Fluid C. Offset D. Xerox

4. The fluid process would be the BEST process to use for reproducing
   A. five copies of a school transcript
   B. fifty copies of a memo
   C. five hundred copies of a form letter
   D. five thousand copies of a chart

5. Which one of the following duplicating processes does NOT require a special master?
   A. Fluid B. Xerox C. Offset D. Stencil

6. Xerox is NOT used for all duplicating jobs because
   A. it produces poor-quality copies
   B. the process is too expensive
   C. preparing the master is too time-consuming
   D. it cannot produce written reports

7. Assume a city agency has 775 office workers.
   If 2 out of 25 office workers were absent on a particular day, how many office workers reported to work on that day?
   A. 713 B. 744 C. 750 D. 773

Questions 8-11.

DIRECTIONS: In Questions 8 through 11, select the choice that is CLOSEST in meaning to the underlined word.

   SAMPLE: This division reviews the fiscal reports of the agency.
   In this sentence, the word *fiscal* means MOST NEARLY
   A. financial B. critical C. basic D. personnel

The correct answer is A, financial, because financial is closest to *fiscal*.

8. A central file eliminates the need to retain duplicate material.
   The word *retain* means MOST NEARLY
   A. keep B. change C. locate D. process

9. Filing is a routine office task.
   Routine means MOST NEARLY
   A. proper B. regular C. simple D. difficult

10. Sometimes a word, phrase, or sentence must be underlined to correct an error. 10._____
Deleted means MOST NEARLY
   A. removed   B. added   C. expanded   D. improved

11. Your supervisor will evaluate your work. 11._____
Evaluate means MOST NEARLY
   A. judge   B. list   C. assign   D. explain

Questions 12-19.

DIRECTIONS: The code table below shows 10 letters with matching numbers. For each Question 12 through 19, there are three sets of letters. Each set of letters is followed by a set of numbers which may or may not match their correct letter according to the code table. For each question, check all three sets of letters and numbers and mark your answer
   A. if no pairs are correctly matched
   B. if only one pair is correctly matched
   C. if only two pairs are correctly matched
   D. if all three pairs are correctly matched

CODE TABLE

T	M	V	D	S	P	R	G	B	H
1	2	3	4	5	6	7	8	9	0

SAMPLE QUESTION: TMVDSP   123456
                   RGBHTM   789011
                   DSPRGB   256789

In the sample question above, the first set of numbers correctly matches its set of letters. But the second and third pairs contain mistakes. In the second pair, M is incorrectly matched with number 1. According to the code table, letter M should be correctly matched with number 2. In the third pair, the letter D is incorrectly matched with number 2. According to the code table, letter D should be correctly matched with number 4. Since only one of the pairs is correctly matched, the answer to this sample question is B.

12. RSBMRM   759262   12._____
     GDSRVH   845730
     VDBRTM   349713

13. TGVSDR   183247   13._____
     SMHRDP   520647
     TRMHSR   172057

14. DSPRGM   456782   14._____
     MVDBHT   234902
     HPMDBT   062491

15.	BVPTRD	936184	15._____
	GDPHMB	807029	
	GMRHMV	827032	

16.	MGVRSH	283750	16._____
	TRDMBS	174295	
	SPRMGV	567283	

17.	SGBSDM	489542	17._____
	MGHPTM	290612	
	MPBMHT	269301	

18.	TDPBHM	146902	18._____
	VPBMRS	369275	
	GDMBHM	842902	

19.	MVPTBV	236194	19._____
	PDRTMB	647128	
	BGTMSM	981232	

Questions 20-25.

DIRECTIONS: In each of Questions 20 through 25, the names of four people are given. For each question, choose as your answer the one of the four names given which should be filed FIRST according to the usual system of alphabetical filing of names, as described in the following paragraph.

In filing names, you must start with the last name. Names are filed in order of the first letter of the last name, then the second letter, etc. Therefore, BAILY would be filed before BROWN, which would be filed before COLT. A name with fewer letters of the same type comes first; i.e., Smith before Smithe. If the last names are the same, the names are filed alphabetically by the first name. If the first name is an initial, a name with an initial would come before a first name that starts with the same letter as the initial. Therefore, I. BROWN would come before IRA BROWN. Finally, if both last name and first name are the same, the name would be filed alphabetically by the middle name, one again an initial coming before a middle name which starts with the same letter as the initial. If there is no middle name at all, the name would come before those with middle initials or names.

SAMPLE QUESTION: A. Lester Daniels
B. William Dancer
C. Nathan Danzig
D. Dan Lester

The last names beginning with D are filed before the last name beginning with L. Since DANIELS, DANCER, and DANZIG all begin with the same three letters, you must look at the fourth letter of the last name to determine which name should be filed first. C comes before I or Z in the alphabet, so DANCER is filed before DANIELS or DANZIG. Therefore, the answer to the above sample question is B.

20. A. Scott Biala B. Mary Byala 20._____
    C. Martin Baylor D. Francis Bauer

21. A. Howard J. Black B. Howard Black 21._____
    C. J. Howard Black D. John H. Black

22. A. Theodora Garth Kingston B. Theodore Barth Kingston 22._____
    C. Thomas Kingston D. Thomas T. Kingston

23. A. Paulette Mary Huerta B. Paul M. Huerta 23._____
    C. Paulette L. Huerta D. Peter A. Huerta

24. A. Martha Hunt Morgan B. Martin Hunt Morgan 24._____
    C. Mary H. Morgan D. Martine H. Morgan

25. A. James T. Meerschaum B. James M. Mershum 25._____
    C. James F. Mearshaum D. James N. Meshum

KEY (CORRECT ANSWERS)

1. C   11. A
2. C   12. B
3. B   13. B
4. B   14. C
5. B   15. A

6. B   16. D
7. A   17. A
8. A   18. D
9. B   19. A
10. A   20. D

21. B
22. B
23. B
24. A
25. C

TEST 3

DIRECTIONS: Each question or incomplete statement is followed by several suggested answers or completions. Select the one that BEST answers the question or completes the statement. *PRINT THE LETTER OF THE CORRECT ANSWER IN THE SPACE AT THE RIGHT.*

1. Which one of the following statements about proper telephone usage is NOT always correct?
   When answering the telephone, you should
   A. know whom you are speaking to
   B. give the caller your undivided attention
   C. identify yourself to the caller
   D. obtain the information the caller wishes before you do your other work

   1._____

2. Assume that, as a member of a worker's safety committee in your agency, you are responsible for encouraging other employees to follow correct safety practices. While you are working on your regular assignment, you observe an employee violating a safety rule.
   Of the following, the BEST action for you to take FIRST is to
   A. speak to the employee about safety practices and order him to stop violating the safety rule
   B. speak to the employee about safety practices and point out the safety rule he is violating
   C. bring the matter up in the next committee meeting
   D. report this violation of the safety rule to the employee's supervisor

   2._____

3. Assume that you have been temporarily assigned by your supervisor to do a job which you do not want to do.
   The BEST action for you to take is to
   A. discuss the job with your supervisor, explaining why you do not want to do it
   B. discuss the job with your supervisor and tell her that you will not do it
   C. ask a co-worker to take your place on this job
   D. do some other job that you like; your supervisor may give the job you do not like to someone else

   3._____

4. Assume that you keep the confidential personnel files of employees in your unit. A friend asks you to obtain some information from the file of one of your co-workers.
   The BEST action to take is to _____ to your friend.
   A. ask the co-worker if you can give the information
   B. ask your supervisor if you can give the information
   C. give the information
   D. refuse to give the information

   4._____

Questions 5-8.

DIRECTIONS: Questions 5 through 8 are to be answered SOLELY on the basis of the information contained in the following passage.

City government is committed to providing a safe and healthy work environment for all city employees. An effective agency safety program reduces accidents by educating employees about the types of careless acts which can cause accidents. Even in an office, accidents can happen. If each employee is aware of possible safety hazards, the number of accidents on the job can be reduced.

Careless use of office equipment can cause accidents and injuries. For example, file cabinet drawers which are filled with papers can be so heavy that the entire cabinet could tip over from the weight of one open drawer.

The bottom drawers of desks and file cabinets should never be left open since employees can easily trip over open drawers and injure themselves.

When reaching for objects on a high shelf, an employee should use a strong, sturdy object such as a stepstool to stand on. Makeshift platforms made out of books, papers, or boxes can easily collapse. Even chairs can slide out from under foot, causing serious injury.

Even at an employee's desk, safety hazards can occur. Frayed or cut wires should be repaired or replaced immediately. Computers which are not firmly anchored to the desk or table could fall, causing injury.

Smoking is one of the major causes of fires in the office. A lighted match or improperly extinguished cigarette thrown into a wastebasket filled with paper could cause a major fire with possible loss of life. Where smoking is permitted, ashtrays should be used. Smoking is particularly dangerous in offices were flammable chemicals are used.

5. The goal of an effective safety program is to 5.____
   A. reduce office accidents
   B. stop employees from smoking on the job
   C. encourage employees to continue their education
   D. eliminate high shelves in offices

6. Desks and file cabinets can become safety hazards when 6.____
   A. their drawers are left open
   B. they are used as wastebaskets
   C. they are makeshift
   D. they are not anchored securely to the floor

7. Smoking is especially hazardous when it occurs 7.____
   A. near exposed wires
   B. in a crowded office
   C. in an area where flammable chemicals are used
   D. where books and papers are stored

8. Accidents are likely to occur when 8.____
   A. employees' desks are cluttered with books and papers
   B. employees are not aware of safety hazards
   C. employees close desk drawers
   D. stepstools are used to reach high objects

9. Assume that part of your job as a worker in the accounting division of a city agency is to answer the telephone.
   When you first answer the telephone, it is LEAST important to tell the caller
   A. your title
   B. your name
   C. the name of your unit
   D. the name of your agency

10. Assume that you are assigned to work as a receptionist, and your duties are to answer phones, greet visitors, and do other general office work. You are busy with a routine job when several visitors approach your desk.
    The BEST action to take is to
    A. ask the visitors to have a seat and assist them after your work is completed
    B. tell the visitors that you are busy and they should return at a more convenient time
    C. stop working long enough to assist the visitors
    D. continue working and wait for the visitors to ask you for assistance

11. Assume that your supervisor has chosen you to take a special course during hours to learn a new payroll procedure. Although you know that you were chosen because of your good work record, a co-worker, who feels that he should have been chosen, has been telling everyone in your unit that the choice was unfair.
    Of the following, the BEST way to handle this situation FIRST is to
    A. suggest to the co-worker that everything in life is unfair
    B. contact your union representative in case your co-worker presents a formal grievance
    C. tell your supervisor about your co-worker's complaints and let her handle the situation
    D. tell the co-worker that you were chosen because of your superior work record

12. Assume that while you are working on an assignment which must be completed quickly, a supervisor from another unit asks you to obtain information for her.
    Of the following, the BEST way to respond to her request is to
    A. tell her to return in an hour since you are busy
    B. give her the names of some people in her own unit who could help her
    C. tell her you are busy and refer her to a co-worker
    D. tell her that you are busy and ask her if she could wait until you finish your assignment

13. A co-worker in your unit is often off from work because of illness. Your supervisor assigns the co-worker's work to you when she is not there. Lately, doing her work has interfered with your own job.
    The BEST action for you to take FIRST is to
    A. discuss the problem with your supervisor
    B. complete your own work before starting your co-worker's work
    C. ask other workers in your unit to assist you
    D. work late in order to get the jobs done

14. During the month of June, 40,587 people attended a city-owned swimming pool. In July, 13,014 more people attended the swimming pool than the number that had attended in June. In August, 39,655 people attended the swimming pool. The TOTAL number of people who attended the swimming pool during the months of June, July, and August was 14.____
    A. 80,242 B. 93,256 C. 133,843 D. 210,382

Questions 15-22.

DIRECTIONS: Questions 15 through 22 test how well you understand what you read. It will be necessary for you to read carefully because your answers to these questions must be based ONLY on the information in the following paragraphs.

The telephone directory is made up of two books. The first book consists of the introductory section and the alphabetical listing of names section. The second book is the classified directory (also known as the yellow pages). Many people who are familiar with one book do not realize how useful the other can be. The efficient office worker should become familiar with both books in order to make the best use of this important source of information.

The introductory section gives general instructions for finding numbers in the alphabetical listing and classified directory. This section also explains how to use the telephone company's many services, including the operator and information services, gives examples of charges for local and long-distance calls, and lists area codes for the entire country. In addition, this section provides a useful zip code map.

The alphabetical listing of names section lists the names, addresses, and telephone numbers of subscribers in an area. Guide names, or *telltales*, are on the top corner of each page. These guide names indicate the first and last name to be found on that page. *Telltales* help locate any particular name quickly. A cross-reference spelling is also given to help locate names which are spelled several different ways. City, state, and federal government agencies are listed under the major government heading. For example, an agency of the federal government would be listed under *United States Government*.

The classified directory, or yellow pages, is a separate book. In this section are advertising services, public transportation line maps, shopping guides, and listings of businesses arranged by the type of product or services they offer. This book is most useful when looking for the name or phone number of a business when all that is known is the type of product offered and the address, or when trying to locate a particular type of business in an area. Businesses listed in the classified directory can usually be found in the alphabetical listing of names section. When the name of the business is known, you will find the address or phone number more quickly in the alphabetical listing of names section.

15. The introductory section provides 15.____
    A. shopping guides B. government listings
    C. business listings D. information services

16. Advertising services would be found in the 16.____
    A. introductory section B. alphabetical listing of names section\
    C. classified directory D. information services

17. According to the information in the above passage for locating government agencies, the Information Office of the Department of Consumer Affairs of New York City government would be alphabetically listed FIRST under
    A. *I* for Information Offices
    B. *D* for Department of Consumer Affairs
    C. *N* for New York City
    D. *G* for government

18. When the name of a business is known, the QUICKEST way to find the phone number is to look in the
    A. classified directory
    B. introductory section
    C. alphabetical listing of name section
    D. advertising service section

19. The QUICKEST way to find the phone number of a business when the type of service a business offers and its address is known is to look in the
    A. classified directory
    B. alphabetical listing of names section
    C. introductory section
    D. information service

20. What is a *telltale*?
    A. An alphabetical listing
    B. A guide name
    C. A map
    D. A cross-reference listing

21. The BEST way to find a postal zip code is to look in the
    A. classified directory
    B. introductory section
    C. alphabetical listing of names section
    D. government heading

22. To help find names which have several different spellings, the telephone directory provides
    A. cross-reference spelling
    B. *telltales*
    C. spelling guides
    D. advertising services

23. Assume that your agency has been given $2,025 to purchase file cabinets. If each file cabinet costs $135, how many file cabinet can your agency purchase?
    A. 8   B. 10   C. 15   D. 16

24. Assume that your unit ordered 14 staplers at a total cost of $30.20 and each stapler cost the same.
    The cost of one stapler was MOST NEARLY
    A. $1.02   B. $1.61   C. $2.16   D. $2.26

25. Assume that you are responsible for counting and recording licensing fees collected by your department. On a particular day, your department collected in fees 40 checks in the amount of $6 each, 80 checks in the amount of $4 each, 45 twenty dollar bills, 30 ten dollar bills, 42 five dollar bills, and 186 one dollar bills.
The TOTAL amount in fees collected on that day was
A. $1,406   B. $1,706   C. $2,156   D. $2,356

26. Assume that you are responsible for your agency's petty cash fund. During the month of February, you pay out 7 $2.00 subway fares and one taxi fare for $10.85. You pay out nothing else from the fund. At the end of February, you count the money left in the fund and find 3 one dollar bills, 4 quarters, 5 dimes, and 4 nickels.
The amount of money you had available in the petty cash fund at the BEGINNING of February was
A. $4.70   B. $16.35   C. $24.85   D. $29.55

27. You overhear your supervisor criticize a co-worker for handling equipment in an unsafe way. You feel that the criticism may be unfair.
Of the following, it would be BEST for you to
A. take your co-worker aside and tell her how you feel about your supervisor's comments
B. interrupt the discussion and defend your co-worker to your supervisor
C. continue working as if you had not overheard the discussion
D. make a list of other workers who have violated safety rules and give it to your supervisor

28. Assume that you have been assigned to work on a long-term project with an employee who is known for being uncooperative.
In beginning to work with this employee, it would be LEAST desirable for you to
A. understand why the person is uncooperative
B. act in a calm manner rather than an emotional manner
C. be appreciative of the co-worker's work
D. report the co-worker's lack of cooperation to your supervisor

29. Assume that you are assigned to sell tickets at a city-owned ice skating rink. An adult ticket costs $4.50, and a children's ticket costs $2.25. At the end of a day, you find that you have sold 36 adult tickets and 80 children's tickets.
The TOTAL amount of money you collected for that day was
A. $244.80   B. $318.00   C. $342.00   D. $348.00

30. If each office worker files 487 index cards in one hour, how many card can 26 office workers file in one hour?
A. 10,662   B. 12,175   C. 12,662   D. 14,266

KEY (CORRECT ANSWERS)

1.	D	11.	C	21.	B
2.	B	12.	D	22.	A
3.	A	13.	A	23.	C
4.	D	14.	C	24.	C
5.	A	15.	D	25.	C
6.	A	16.	C	26.	D
7.	C	17.	C	27.	C
8.	B	18.	C	28.	D
9.	A	19.	A	29.	C
10.	C	20.	B	30.	C

EXAMINATION SECTION

TEST 1

DIRECTIONS: Each question or incomplete statement is followed by several suggested answers or completions. Select the one that BEST answers the question or completes the statement. *PRINT THE LETTER OF THE CORRECT ANSWER IN THE SPACE AT THE RIGHT.*

1. The one of the following that is MOST advisable to do before transcribing your dictation notes is to
    A. check the syllabification of long words for typing purposes
    B. edit your notes
    C. number the pages of dictation
    D. sort them by the kind of typing format required

    1._____

2. As a secretary, the one of the following which is LEAST important in writing a letter under your own signature is
    A. the accuracy of the information
    B. the appropriateness of the language
    C. the reason for the letter
    D. your supervisor's approval of the final copy

    2._____

3. In a typed letter, the reference line is used
    A. for identification purposes on typed pages of more than one page
    B. to indicate under what heading the copy of the letter should be filed
    C. to indicate who dictated the letter and who typed it
    D. to make the subject of the letter prominent by typing it a single space below the salutation

    3._____

Questions 4-5:

DIRECTIONS: For questions 4 and 5, choose the letter of the sentence that BEST and MOST clearly expresses its meaning.

4.
    A. It has always been the practice of this office to effectuate recruitment of prospective employees from other departments.
    B. This office has always made a practice of recruiting prospective employees from other departments.
    C. Recruitment of prospective employees from other departments has always been a practice which has been implemented by this office.
    D. Implementation of the policy of recruitment of prospective employees from other departments has always been a practice of this office.

    4._____

5.
   A. These employees are assigned to the level of work evidenced by their efforts and skills during the training period.
   B. The level of work to which these employees is assigned is decided upon on the basis of the efforts and skills evidenced by them during the period in which they were trained.
   C. Assignment of these employees is made on the basis of the level of work their efforts and skills during the training period has evidenced.
   D. These employees are assigned to a level of work their efforts and skills during the training period have evidenced.

5._____

6. An office assistant was asked to mail a duplicated report of 100 pages to a professor in an out-of-town university. The professor sending the report dictated a short letter that he wanted to mail with the report.
   Of the following, the MOST inexpensive proper means of sending these two items would be to send the report
   A. and the letter first class
   B. by parcel post and the letter separately by air mail
   C. and the letter by parcel post
   D. by parcel post and attach to the package an envelope with first-class postage in which is enclosed the letter

6._____

7. Plans are underway to determine the productivity of the typists who work in a central office. Of the procedures listed, the one generally considered the MOST accurate for finding out the typists' output is to
   A. keep a record of how much typing is done over specified periods of time
   B. ask each typist how fast she types when she is doing a great deal of word processing
   C. give each typist a timed test during a specified period
   D. ask the supervisor to estimate the typing speed of each subordinate

7._____

8. Assume that an executive regularly receives the four types of mail listed below.
   As a general rule, the executive's secretary should arrange the mail from top to bottom so that the top items are
   A. advertisements
   B. airmail letters
   C. business letters
   D. unopened personal letters

8._____

9. An office assistant in transcribing reports and letters from dictation should MOST generally assume that
   A. the transcript should be exactly what was dictated so there is little need to check any details
   B. the dictated material is merely an idea of what the dictator wanted to say so changes should be made to improve any part of the dictation
   C. there may be some slight changes, but essentially the transcription is to be a faithful copy of what was dictated
   D. the transcript is merely a very rough draft and should be typed quickly so that the dictator can review it and make changes preliminary to having the final copy typed

9._____

10. The one of the following which generally is the CHIEF disadvantage of using office machines in place of human workers in office work is that the machines are
    A. slower
    B. less accurate
    C. more costly
    D. less flexible

10._____

11. An office assistant in a New York City college is asked to place a call to a prospective visiting professor in Los Angeles. It is 1 p.m. in New York (EST). The time in Los Angeles is
    A. 9 a.m.   B. 10 a.m.   C. 4 p.m.   D. 5 p.m.

11._____

12. An office assistant is instructed to send a copy of a report to a professor located in a building across campus. The fastest and most efficient way for this report to reach the professor is by
    A. sending a messenger to hand-deliver it to the professor's office
    B. sending it via fax to the main office of the professor's department
    C. e-mailing it to the professor
    D. dictating the contents of the report to the professor over the phone

12._____

13. An office assistant is in the process of typing the forms for recommendation for promotion for a member of the faculty who is away for a week. She notes that two books of which he is the author are listed without dates.
Of the following, the procedure she should BEST follow at this point generally is to
    A. postpone doing the job until the professor returns to campus the following week
    B. type the material omitting the books
    C. check the professor's office for copies of the books and obtain the correct data
    D. call the professor's wife and ask her when the books were published

13._____

14. An office has introduced work standards for all of the employees. 14._____
Of the following, it is MOST likely that use of such standards would tend to
   A. make it more difficult to determine numbers of employees needed
   B. lead to a substantial drop in morale among all of the employees
   C. reduce the possibility of planning to meet emergencies
   D. reduce uncertainty about the costs of doing tasks

15. Of the following clerical errors, the one which probably is LEAST important is 15._____
   A. adding 543 instead of 548 to a bookkeeping account
   B. putting the wrong code on a data processing card
   C. recording a transaction on the record of Henry Smith instead of on the record of Harry Smith
   D. writing John Murpfy instead of John Murphy when addressing an envelope

16. Of the following errors, the one which probably is MOST important is 16._____
   A. writing "they're" instead of "their" in an office memo
   B. misplacing a decimal point on a sales invoice
   C. forgetting to write the date on a note for a supervisor
   D. sending an e-mail to a misspelled e-mail address

17. The chairman of an academic department tells an office assistant that a meeting of the faculty is to be held four weeks from the current date. 17._____
Of the following responsibilities, the office assistant is MOST frequently held responsible for
   A. planning the agenda of the meeting
   B. presiding over the conduct of the meeting
   C. reserving the meeting room and notifying the members
   D. initiating all formal resolutions

18. Of the following, a centralized filing system is LEAST suitable for filing 18._____
   A. material which is confidential in nature
   B. routine correspondence
   C. periodic reports of the divisions of the department
   D. material used by several divisions of the department

19. A misplaced record is a lost record. 19._____
Of the following, the MOST valid implication of this statement in regard to office work is that
   A. all records in an office should be filed in strict alphabetical order
   B. accuracy in filing is essential
   C. only one method of filing should be used throughout the office
   D. files should be locked when not in use

20. When typing names or titles on a roll of folder labels, the one of the following which is MOST important to do is to type the caption
    A. as it appears on the papers to be placed in the folder
    B. in capital letters
    C. in exact indexing or filing order
    D. so that it appears near the bottom of the folder tab when the label is attached

21. A professor at a Boston university asks an office assistant to place a call to a fellow professor in San Francisco. The MOST appropriate local time for the assistant to place the call to the professor in California, given the time difference, would be
    A. 8:30 a.m.   B. 10:00 a.m.   C. 11:30 a.m.   D. 1:30 p.m.

22. When typing the rough draft of a report, the computer application you would use is
    A. Excel
    B. Word
    C. PowerPoint
    D. Internet Explorer

23. Which of the following is the BEST and most appropriate way to proofread and edit a report before submitting it to a supervisor for review?
    A. Scan the report with the program's spell check feature
    B. Proof the report yourself, then ask another office assistant to read the report over as well until it is finished
    C. Give the report to another office assistant who is more skilled at proofreading
    D. Use the spell checker, then scan the report yourself as many times as needed in order to pick up any additional errors

24. The one of the following situations in which it would be MOST justifiable for an office to use standard or form paragraphs in its business letters is when
    A. a large number of similar letters is to be sent
    B. the letters are to be uniform in length and appearance
    C. it is desired to reduce typing errors in correspondence
    D. the office is to carry on a lengthy correspondence with an individual

25. Of the following, the MOST important factor in determining whether or not an office filing system is effective is that the
    A. information in the files is legible
    B. records in the files are used frequently
    C. information in the files is accurate
    D. records in the files can be located readily

KEY (CORRECT ANSWERS)

1. B	11. B	21. D
2. D	12. C	22. B
3. C	13. C	23. D
4. B	14. D	24. A
5. A	15. D	25. D
6. D	16. B	
7. A	17. C	
8. D	18. A	
9. C	19. B	
10. D	20. C	

TEST 2

DIRECTIONS: Each question or incomplete statement is followed by several suggested answers or completions. Select the one that BEST answers the question or completes the statement. *PRINT THE LETTER OF THE CORRECT ANSWER IN THE SPACE AT THE RIGHT.*

1. For the office assistant whose duties include frequent recording and transcription of minutes of formal meetings, the one of the following reference works generally considered to be MOST useful is
    A. *Robert's Rules of Order*
    B. *Bartlett's Familiar Quotations*
    C. *World Almanac and Book of Facts*
    D. *Conway's Reference*

   1._____

2. Of the following statements about the numeric system of filing, the one which is CORRECT is that it
    A. is the least accurate of all methods of filing
    B. eliminates the need for cross-referencing
    C. allows for very limited expansion
    D. requires a separate index

   2._____

3. When more than one name or subject is involved in a piece of correspondence to be filed, the office assistant should GENERALLY
    A. prepare a cross-reference sheet
    B. establish a geographical filing system
    C. prepare out-guides
    D. establish a separate index card file for noting such correspondence

   3._____

4. A tickler file is MOST generally used for
    A. identification of material contained in a numeric file
    B. maintenance of a current listing of telephone numbers
    C. follow-up of matters requiring future attention
    D. control of records borrowed or otherwise removed from the files

   4._____

5. In filing, the name Ms. *Ann Catalana-Moss* should GENERALLY be indexed as
    A. Moss, Catalana, Ann (Ms.)
    B. Catalana-Moss, Ann (Ms.)
    C. Ann Catalana-Moss (Ms.)
    D. Moss-Catalana, Ann (Ms.)

   5._____

6. An office assistant has a set of four cards, each of which contains one of the following names.
   In alphabetic filing, the FIRST of the cards to be filed is
   A. Ms. Alma John
   B. Mrs. John (Patricia) Edwards
   C. John-Edward School Supplies, Inc.
   D. John H. Edwards

7. Generally, of the following, the name to be filed FIRST in an alphabetical filing system is
   A. Diane Maestro
   B. Diana McElroy
   C. James Mackell
   D. James McKell

8. After checking several times, you are unable to locate a student record in its proper file drawer. The file drawer in question is used constantly by many members of the staff.
   In this situation, the NEXT step you should take in locating the missing record is to
   A. ask another worker to look through the file drawer
   B. determine if there is another copy of the record filed in a different place
   C. find out if the record has been removed by another staff member
   D. wait a day or two and see if the record turns up

9. It is MOST important that an enclosure which is to be mailed with a letter should be put in an envelope so that
   A. any printing on the enclosure will not be visible through the address side of the envelope
   B. it is obvious that there is an enclosure inside the envelope
   C. the enclosure takes up less space than the letter
   D. the person who opens the envelope will pull out both the letter and the enclosure

10. Suppose that one of the student aides with whom you work suggests a change in the filing procedure. He is sure the change will result in increased rates of filing among the other employees.
    The one of the following which you should do FIRST is to
    A. ask him to demonstrate his method in order to determine if he files more quickly than the other employees
    B. ask your supervisor if you may make a change in the filing procedure
    C. ignore the aide's suggestion since he is not a filing expert
    D. tell him to show his method to the other employees and to encourage them to use it

11. It is generally advisable to leave at least six inches of working space in a file drawer. This procedure is MOST useful in
    A. decreasing the number of filing errors
    B. facilitating the sorting of documents and folders
    C. maintaining a regular program of removing inactive records
    D. preventing folders and papers from being torn

12. Assume that a dictator is briefly interrupted because of a telephone call or other similar matter (no more than three minutes).
    Of the following tasks, the person taking the dictation should NORMALLY use the time to
    A. re-read notes already recorded
    B. tidy the dictator's desk
    C. check the accuracy of the dictator's desk files
    D. return to her own desk to type the dictated material

13. When typing a preliminary draft of a report, the one of the following which you should generally NOT do is
    A. erase typing errors and deletions rather than cross them out
    B. leave plenty of room at the top, bottom and sides of each page
    C. make only the number of copies that you are asked to make
    D. type double or triple space

14. The BEST way for a receptionist to deal with a situation in which she must leave her desk for a long time is to
    A. ask someone to take her place while she is away
    B. leave a note or sign on her desk which indicates the time she will return
    C. take a chance that no one will arrive while she is gone and leave her desk unattended
    D. tell a coworker to ask any visitors that arrive to wait until she returns

15. Suppose that two individuals come up to your desk at the same time. One of them asks you for the location of the nearest public phone. After you answer the question, you turn to the second person who asks you the same question.
    The one of the following actions that would be BEST for you to take in this situation is to
    A. ignore the second person since he obviously overheard your first answer
    B. point out that you just answered the same question and quickly repeat the information
    C. politely repeat the information to the second individual
    D. tell the second person to follow the first to the public telephone

16. Which of the following names should be filed FIRST in an alphabetical filing system?
    A. Anthony Aarvedsen
    B. William Aaron
    C. Denise Aron
    D. A.J. Arrington

17. New material added to a file folder should USUALLY be inserted
    A. in the order of importance (the most important in front)
    B. in the order of importance (the most important in back)
    C. chronologically (most recent in front)
    D. chronologically (most recent in back)

18. An individual is looking for a name in the White Pages of a telephone directory.
    Which of the following BEST describes the system of filing found there?
    A. alphabetic
    B. sequential
    C. locator
    D. index

19. The MAIN purpose of a tickler file is to
    A. help prevent overlooking matters that require future attention
    B. check on adequacy of past performance
    C. pinpoint responsibility for recurring daily tasks
    D. reduce the volume of material kept in general files

20. Which of the following BEST describes the process of *reconciling* a bank statement?
    A. Analyzing the nature of the expenditures made by the office during the preceding month
    B. Comparing the statement of the bank with the banking records maintained in the office
    C. Determining the liquidity position by reading the bank statement carefully
    D. Checking the service charges noted on the bank statement

21. From the viewpoint of preserving agency or institutional funds, the LEAST acceptable method for making a payment is a check made out to
    A. cash
    B. a company
    C. an individual
    D. a partnership

22. Listed below are four of the steps in the process of preparing correspondence for filing.
    If they were to be put in logical sequence, the SECOND step would be
    A. preparing cross-reference sheets or cards
    B. coding the correspondence using a classification system
    C. sorting the correspondence in the order to be filed
    D. checking for follow-up action required and preparing a follow-up slip

23. The process of *justifying* typed copy involves laying out the copy so that
    A. each paragraph appears to be approximately the same size
    B. no long words are broken up at the end of a line
    C. the right and left hand margins are even
    D. there is enough room to enter proofreading marks at the end of each line

24. The MOST important reason for a person in charge of a petty cash fund to obtain receipts for payments is that this practice would tend to
    A. decrease robberies by delivery personnel
    B. eliminate the need to keep a record of petty cash expenditures
    C. prove that the fund has been used properly
    D. provide a record of the need for cash in the daily operations of the office

25. You should GENERALLY replenish a petty cash fund
    A. at regularly established intervals
    B. each time you withdraw a sum
    C. when the amount of cash gets below a certain specified amount
    D. when the fund is completely empty

KEY (CORRECT ANSWERS)

1. A	11. D	21. A
2. D	12. A	22. A
3. A	13. A	23. C
4. C	14. A	24. C
5. B	15. C	25. C
6. D	16. B	
7. C	17. C	
8. C	18. A	
9. D	19. A	
10. A	20. B	

EXAMINATION SECTION
TEST 1

DIRECTIONS: Each question or incomplete statement is followed by several suggested answers or completions. Select the one that BEST answers the question or completes the statement. *PRINT THE LETTER OF THE CORRECT ANSWER IN THE SPACE AT THE RIGHT.*

1. In considering a new word processing system for a regional office, which of the following would MOST likely be the MOST important consideration in making a decision?

    A. Ease of operation
    B. Friendliness of service technicians
    C. Availability of service technicians
    D. Capacity of the system to meet the unit's word processing needs

    1._____

2. Your supervisor is out of town for several days and has asked you to act as supervisor in his absence. An employee in the unit comes to you and complains that the supervisor has been dividing the workload unfairly.
Of the following, the MOST appropriate action for you to take is

    A. defend the actions of your supervisor
    B. encourage the employee to file a grievance
    C. listen to the employee attentively
    D. explain to the employee that you have no authority to handle the situation

    2._____

3. A principal stenographer still on probation is instructed to supervise and coordinate the completion of a large word processing project. Her supervisor asks her how long she thinks the project will take. The principal stenographer gives her supervisor an estimate that is two days longer than she actually thinks the project will take to complete. The project is completed two days earlier, and the principal stenographer is congratulated by her supervisor for her efforts.
In purposely overestimating the time required to complete the project, the principal stenographer showed

    A. *good* judgment because it helped her appear very efficient
    B. *good* judgment because it helps keep unrealistic supervisors from expecting too much
    C. *poor* judgment because plans and schedules of other components of the project may have been based on her false estimate
    D. *poor* judgment because she should have used the extra time to further check and, proofread the work

    3._____

4. Which of the following would MOST likely be the MOST important in providing support to one's supervisor?

    A. Screening annoying phone calls
    B. Reviewing and forwarding articles and publications that may be of interest to your supervisor
    C. Correctly transmitting instructions from the supervisor to appropriate staff members
    D. Reviewing outgoing correspondence for proper grammatical usage and clarity

    4._____

5. While you are on the telephone answering a question about your agency, a visitor comes to your desk and starts to ask you a question. There is no emergency or urgency in either situation, that of the phone call or that of answering the visitor's question.
   In this case, you should

   A. excuse yourself to the person on the telephone and tell the visitor that you will be with him or her as soon as you have finished on the phone
   B. explain to the person on the phone that you have a visitor and must shorten the conversation
   C. continue to talk with the person on the phone while looking up occasionally at the visitor to let him or her know that you know he or she is there
   D. continue to talk with the person on the telephone until you are finished and then let the visitor know that you're sorry to have kept him or her waiting

6. Your supervisor is out of town on vacation for one week, and asks you to act as supervisor in her absence. The second day she is gone a very important, complex budgetary form, which must be responded to in ten days, arrives in your unit.
   Of the following, it would be BEST if you

   A. filled out the form and submitted it as soon as possible
   B. read the form over, did any time-consuming research that might be needed, and then gave the uncompleted form to your supervisor as soon as she returned
   C. asked for help from your supervisor's supervisor in completing the form
   D. tried to contact your supervisor for advice

7. Of the following, which would MOST likely be of the highest priority?
   The typing of

   A. a grant proposal due next week
   B. new addresses onto a mailing list for a future mailing
   C. a payroll form for a new employee that needs to be submitted immediately
   D. a memorandum from the Commissioner to all employees regarding new procedures

8. Your office is moving to a new location.
   Of the following, it would be MOST important to ensure that

   A. others will know your office's new address and phone number
   B. the new office space is comfortable
   C. your supervisor is happy with his or her new office space
   D. the move itself goes smoothly

9. Of the following, which would generally be considered the LEAST desirable?

   A. Accidentally disconnecting an executive from an important phone call
   B. Ordering the wrong back-up part for a copying machine
   C. Misplacing several hundred dollars worth of personal checks payable to your department
   D. Misplacing a memorandum that needs to be typed

10. Your supervisor has told you not to let anyone disturb her for the rest of the morning unless absolutely necessary because she has some urgent work to complete. The department head telephones and asks to speak to her.
    The BEST course of action for you to take is to

    A. ask the department head if he or she can leave a message
    B. ask your supervisor if she can take the call
    C. tell the department head that your supervisor is out
    D. let your supervisor know that her instructions have put you in a difficult position

11. Which of the following would be MOST likely to contribute to efficiency in the operation of an office?

    A. A new computer system is instituted in an office.
    B. The employees are paid well.
    C. Procedures and practices are studied for any redundant operations.
    D. A supervisor delegates work.

12. You are at work at your desk on a special project when a visitor approaches you. You cannot interrupt your work to take care of this person.
    Of the following, the BEST and MOST courteous way of handling this situation is to

    A. avoid looking up from your work until you are finished with what you are doing
    B. tell the visitor that you will not be able to assist him or her for quite some time
    C. refer the individual to another employee who can take care of him or her right away
    D. chat with the individual while you continue to work

13. Which of the following would MOST likely be of the highest priority?
    A(n)

    A. annual report due next month
    B. irate member of the public who is standing at your desk
    C. important financial report requested by the Commissioner
    D. memorandum to all employees outlining very important new policy needs to be typed and distributed immediately

14. Someone uses *special pull* to obtain the services of your unit at the last minute. You and the four employees you supervise have done everything you could do to provide good service, and you feel things have gone very well. The client is not pleased, however, and enters your office and begins screaming at you and the other employees present.
    Of the following, it would be BEST if you

    A. ignored the person
    B. tried to calm the person down
    C. asked the person to leave the office
    D. called your supervisor in to help handle the situation

15. Your supervisor is on vacation for two weeks, and you have been asked to fill in for her. Your office is very busy, and there is a strict procedure for filling requests. Leslie from Unit X wants something completed immediately. You don't feel this is possible or reasonable, and politely explain why to Leslie. Leslie becomes very angry and says that she will complain to your supervisor about your uncooperative behavior as soon as your supervisor returns.
Of the following, it would be BEST if you

   A. filled Leslie's request
   B. reported Leslie to her supervisor
   C. complained to your supervisor about the situation as soon as she returned
   D. stood by your decision once you determined it was correct

---

KEY (CORRECT ANSWERS)

1. D	6. B	11. C
2. C	7. C	12. C
3. C	8. A	13. B
4. C	9. C	14. B
5. A	10. B	15. D

CLERICAL ABILITIES TEST
EXAMINATION SECTION
TEST 1

DIRECTIONS: Each question or incomplete statement is followed by several suggested answers or completions. Select the one that BEST answers the question or completes the statement. *PRINT THE LETTER OF THE CORRECT ANSWER IN THE SPACE AT THE RIGHT.*

Questions 1-10.

DIRECTIONS: Questions 1 through 10 consist of lines of names, dates, and numbers. For each question, you are to choose the option (A, B, C, or D) in Column II which EXACTLY matches the information in Column I. *PRINT THE LETTER OF THE CORRECT ANSWER IN THE SPACE AT THE RIGHT.*

SAMPLE QUESTION

Column I
Schneider 11/16/75 581932

Column II
A. Schneider 11/16/75 518932
B. Schneider 11/16/75 581932
C. Schnieder 11/16/75 581932
D. Shnieder 11/16/75 518932

The correct answer is B. Only Option B shows the name, date, and number exactly as they are in Column I. Option A has a mistake in the number. Option C has a mistake in the name. Option D has a mistake in the name and in the number. Now answer Questions 1 through 10 in the same manner.

   Column I
1. Johnston 12/26/74 659251

   Column II
   A. Johnson 12/23/74 659251
   B. Johston 12/26/74 659251
   C. Johnston 12/26/74 695251
   D. Johnston 12/26/74 659251

1.____

2. Allison 1/26/75 9939256

   A. Allison 1/26/75 9939256
   B. Alisson 1/26/75 9939256
   C. Allison 1/26/76 9399256
   D. Allison 1/26/75 9993356

2.____

3. Farrell 2/12/75 361251

   A. Farell 2/21/75 361251
   B. Farrell 2/12/75 361251
   C. Farrell 2/21/75 361251
   D. Farrell 2/12/75 361151

3.____

4. Guerrero 4/28/72 105689
   A. Guererro 4/28/72 105689
   B. Guererro 4/28/72 105986
   C. Guerrero 4/28/72 105869
   D. Guerrero 4/28/72 105689

4.____

5. McDonnell 6/05/73 478215
   A. McDonnell 6/15/73 478215
   B. McDonnell 6/05/73 478215
   C. McDonnell 6/05/73 472815
   D. MacDonell 6/05/73 478215

5.____

6. Shepard 3/31/71 075421
   A. Sheperd 3/31/71 075421
   B. Shepard 3/13/71 075421
   C. Shepard 3/31/71 075421
   D. Shepard 3/13/71 075241

6.____

7. Russell 4/01/69 031429
   A. Russell 4/01/69 031429
   B. Russell 4/10/69 034129
   C. Russell 4/10/69 031429
   D. Russell 4/01/69 034129

7.____

8. Phillips 10/16/68 961042
   A. Philipps 10/16/68 961042
   B. Phillips 10/16/68 960142
   C. Phillips 10/16/68 961042
   D. Philipps 10/16/68 916042

8.____

9. Campbell 11/21/72 624856
   A. Campbell 11/21/72 624856
   B. Campbell 11/21/72 624586
   C. Campbell 11/21/72 624686
   D. Campbel 11/21/72 624856

9.____

10. Patterson 9/18/71 76199176
   A. Patterson 9/18/72 76191976
   B. Patterson 9/18/71 76199176
   C. Patterson 9/18/72 76199176
   D. Patterson 9/18/71 76919176

10.____

Questions 11-15.

DIRECTIONS: Questions 11 through 15 consist of groups of numbers and letters which you are to compare. For each question, you are to choose the option (A, B, C, or D) in Column I which EXACTLY matches the group of numbers and letters given in Column I.

SAMPLE QUESTION

Column I
B92466

Column II
A. B92644
B. B94266
C. A92466
D. B92466

The correct answer is D. Only Option D in Column II shows the group of numbers and letters EXACTLY as it appears in Column I. Now answer Questions 11 through 15 in the same manner.

	Column I		Column II	
11.	925AC5	A.	952CA5	11._____
		B.	925AC5	
		C.	952AC5	
		D.	925CA6	
12.	Y006925	A.	Y060925	12._____
		B.	Y006295	
		C.	Y006529	
		D.	Y006925	
13.	J236956	A.	J236956	13._____
		B.	J326965	
		C.	J239656	
		D.	J932656	
14.	AB6952	A.	AB6952	14._____
		B.	AB9625	
		C.	AB9652	
		D.	AB6925	
15.	X259361	A.	X529361	15._____
		B.	X259631	
		C.	X523961	
		D.	X259361	

Questions 16-25.

DIRECTIONS: Each of questions 16 through 25 consists of three lines of code letters and three lines of numbers. The numbers on each line should correspond with the code letters on the same line in accordance with the table below.

Code Letter	S	V	W	A	Q	M	X	E	G	K
Corresponding Number	0	1	2	3	4	5	5	7	8	9

On some of the lines, an error exists in the coding. Compare the letters and numbers in each question carefully. If you find an error or errors on:
    only one of the lines in the question, mark your answer A;
    any two lines in the question, mark your answer B;
    all three lines in the question, mark your answer C;
    none of the lines in the question, mark your answer D.

SAMPLE QUESTION

WQGKSXG	2489068
XEKVQMA	6591453
KMAESXV	9527061

In the above sample, the first line is correct since each code letter listed has the correct corresponding number. On the second line, an error exists because code letter E should have the number 7 instead of the number 5. On the third line, an error exists because the code letter A should have the number 3 instead of the number 2. Since there are errors in two of the three lines, the correct answer is B. Now answer Questions 16 through 25 in the same manner.

16. SWQEKGA   0247983   16.____
      KEAVSXM   9731065
      SSAXGKQ   0036894

17. QAMKMVS   4259510   17.____
      MGGEASX   5897306
      KSWMKWS   9125920

18. WKXQWVE   2964217   18.____
      QKXXQVA   4966413
      AWMXGVS   3253810

19. GMMKASE   8559307   19.____
      AWVSKSW   3210902
      QAVSVGK   4310189

20. XGKQSMK   6894049   20.____
      QSVKEAS   4019730
      GSMXKMV   8057951

21. AEKMWSG   3195208   21.____
      MKQSVQK   5940149
      XGQAEVW   6843712

22. XGMKAVS   6858310   22.____
      SKMAWEQ   0953174
      GVMEQSA   8167403

23. VQSKAVE   1489317   23.____
      WQGKAEM   2489375
      MEGKAWQ   5689324

24. XMQVSKG   6541098   24.____
      QMEKEWS   4579720
      KMEVGKG   9571983

5 (#1)

25. GKVAMEW 88912572 25._____
  AXMVKAE 3651937
  KWAGMAV 9238531

Questions 26-35.

DIRECTIONS: Each of Questions 26 through 35 consists of a column of figures. For each question, add the column of figures and choose the correct answer from the four choices given.

26. 5,665.43 26._____
  2,356.69
  6,447.24
  <u>7,239.65</u>

  A. 20,698.01 B. 21,709.01
  C. 21,718.01 D. 22,609.01

27. 817,209.55 27._____
  264,354.29
   82,368.76
  <u>849,964.89</u>

  A. 1,893.977.49 B. 1,989,988.39
  C. 2,009,077.39 D. 2,013,897.49

28. 156,366.89 28._____
  249,973.23
  823,229.49
   <u>56,869.45</u>

  A. 1,286,439.06 B. 1,287,521.06
  C. 1,297,539.06 D. 1,296,421.06

29. 23,422.15 29._____
  149,696.24
  238,377.53
   86,289.79
  <u>505,533.63</u>

  A. 989,229.34 B. 999,879.34
  C. 1,003,330.34 D. 1,023,329.34

30. 2,468,926.70
     656,842.28
     49,723.15
     832,369.59

    A. 3,218,062.72   B. 3,808,092.72
    C. 4,007,861.72   D. 4,818,192.72

31.   524,201.52
     7,775,678.51
     8,345,299.63
    40,628,898.08
    31,374,670.07

    A. 88,646,647.81   B. 88,646,747.91
    C. 88,648,647.91   D. 88,648,747.81

32. 6,824,829.40
       682,482.94
     5,542,015.27
       775,678.51
     7,732,507.25

    A. 21,557,513.37   B. 21,567,513.37
    C. 22,567,503.37   D. 22,567,513.37

33. 22,109,405.58
      6,097,093.43
      5,050,073.99
      8,118,050.05
      4,313,980.82

    A. 45,688,593.87   B. 45,688,603.87
    C. 45,689,593.87   D. 45,689,603.87

34. 79,324,114.19
     99,848,129.74
     43,331,653.31
     41,610,207.14

    A. 264,114,104.38   B. 264,114,114.38
    C. 265,114,114.38   D. 265,214,104.38

35. 33,729,653.94
    5,959,342.58
    26,052,715.47
    4,452,669.52
    7,079,953.59

   A. 76,374,334.10
   B. 76,375,334.10
   C. 77,274,335.10
   D. 77,275,335.10

35._____

Questions 36-40.

DIRECTIONS: Each of Questions 36 through 40 consists of a single number in Column I and four options in Column II. For each question, you are to choose the option (A, B, C, or D) in Column II which EXACTLY matches the number in Column I.

SAMPLE QUESTION

Column I
5965121

Column II
A. 5956121
B. 5965121
C. 5966121
D. 5965211

The correct answer is B. Only Option B shows the number EXACTLY as it appears in Column I. Now answer Questions 36 through 40 in the same manner.

	Column I	Column II	
36.	9643242	A. 9643242 B. 9462342 C. 9642442 D. 9463242	36._____
37.	3572477	A. 3752477 B. 3725477 C. 3572477 D. 3574277	37._____
38.	5276101	A. 5267101 B. 5726011 C. 5271601 D. 5276101	38._____
39.	4469329	A. 4496329 B. 4469329 C. 4496239 D. 4469239	39._____

40. 2326308   A. 2236308   40._____
                      B. 2233608
                      C. 2326308
                      D. 2323608

KEY (CORRECT ANSWERS)

1.	D	11.	B	21.	A	31.	D
2.	A	12.	D	22.	C	32.	A
3.	B	13.	A	23.	B	33.	B
4.	D	14.	A	24.	D	34.	A
5.	B	15.	D	25.	A	35.	C
6.	C	16.	D	26.	B	36.	A
7.	A	17.	C	27.	D	37.	C
8.	C	18.	A	28.	A	38.	D
9.	A	19.	D	29.	C	39.	B
10.	B	20.	B	30.	C	40.	C

TEST 2

DIRECTIONS: Each question or incomplete statement is followed by several suggested answers or completions. Select the one that BEST answers the question or completes the statement. *PRINT THE LETTER OF THE CORRECT ANSWER IN THE SPACE AT THE RIGHT.*

Questions 1-5.

DIRECTIONS: Each of Questions 1 through 5 consists of a name and a dollar amount. In each question, the name and dollar amount in Column II should be an EXACT copy of the name and dollar amount in Column I. If there is:
    a mistake only in the name, mark your answer A;
    a mistake only in the dollar amount, mark your answer B;
    a mistake in both the name and the dollar amount, mark your answer C;
    no mistake in either the name or the dollar amount, mark your answer D.

SAMPLE QUESTION

Column I	Column II
George Peterson	George Petersson
$125.50	$125.50

Compare the name and dollar amount in Column II with the name and dollar amount in Column I. The name *Petersson* in Column II is spelled *Peterson* in Column I. The amount is the same in both columns. Since there is a mistake only in the name, the answer to the sample question is A. Now answer Questions 1 through 5 in the same manner.

	Column I	Column II	
1.	Susanne Shultz $3440	Susanne Schultz $3440	1.____
2.	Anibal P. Contrucci $2121.61	Anibel P. Contrucci $2112.61	2.____
3.	Eugenio Mendoza $12.45	Eugenio Mendozza $12.45	3.____
4.	Maurice Gluckstadt $4297	Maurice Gluckstadt $4297	4.____
5.	John Pampellonne $4656.94	John Pammpellonne $4566.94	5.____

Questions 6-11.

DIRECTIONS: Each of Questions 6 through 11 consist of a set of names and addresses, which you are to compare. In each question, the name and addresses in Column II should be an EXACT copy of the name and address in Column I. If there is:
- a mistake only in the name, mark your answer A;
- a mistake only in the address, mark your answer B;
- a mistake in both the name and address, mark your answer C;
- no mistake in either the name or address, mark your answer D.

SAMPLE QUESTION

Column I	Column II
Michael Filbert	Michael Filbert
456 Reade Street	645 Reade Street
New York, N.Y. 10013	New York, N.Y. 10013

Since there is a mistake only in the address (the street number should be 456 instead of 645), the answer to the sample question is B. Now answer Questions 6 through 11 in the same manner.

	Column I	Column II	
6.	Hilda Goettelmann 55 Lenox Rd. Brooklyn, N.Y. 11226	Hilda Goetteman 55 Lenox Ave. Brooklyn, N.Y. 11226	6.____
7.	Arthur Sherman 2522 Batchelder St. Brooklyn, N.Y. 11235	Arthur Sharman 2522 Batcheder St. Brooklyn, N.Y. 11253	7.____
8.	Ralph Barnett 300 West 28 Street New York, New York 10001	Ralph Barnett 300 West 28 Street New York, New York 10001	8.____
9.	George Goodwin 135 Palmer Avenue Staten Island, New York 10302	George Godwin 135 Palmer Avenue Staten Island, New York 10302	9.____
10.	Alonso Ramirez 232 West 79 Street New York, N.Y. 10024	Alonso Ramirez 223 West 79 Street New York, N.Y. 10024	10.____
11.	Cynthia Graham 149-34 83 Street Howard Beach, N.Y. 11414	Cynthia Graham 149-35 83 Street Howard Beach, N.Y. 11414	11.____

Questions 12-20.

DIRECTIONS: Questions 12 through 20 are problems in subtraction. For each question do the subtraction and select your answer from the four choices given.

12. 232,921.85
    -179,587.68

    A. 52,433.17   B. 52,434.17
    C. 53,334.17   D. 53,343,17

    12.____

13. 5,531,876.29
    -3,897,158.36

    A. 1,634,717.93   B. 1,644,718.93
    C. 1,734,717.93   D. 1,7234,718.93

    13.____

14. 1,482,658.22
    -937,925.76

    A. 544,633.46   B. 544,732.46
    C. 545,632.46   D. 545,732.46

    14.____

15. 937,828.17
    -259,673.88

    A. 678,154.29   B. 679,154.29
    C. 688,155.39   D. 699,155.39

    15.____

16. 760,412.38
    -263,465.95

    A. 496,046.43   B. 496,946.43
    C. 496,956.43   D. 497,046.43

    16.____

17. 3,203,902.26
    -2,933,087.96

    A. 260,814.30   B. 269,824.30
    C. 270,814.30   D. 270,824.30

    17.____

18. 1,023,468.71
    -934,678.88

    A. 88,780.83   B. 88,789.83
    C. 88,880.83   D. 88,889.83

    18.____

19. 831,549.47
    -772,814.78

    A. 58,734.69   B. 58,834.69
    C. 59,735.69   D. 59,834.69

20. 6,306,181.74
    -3,617,376.99

    A. 2,687,904.99   B. 2,688,904.99
    C. 2,689,804.99   D. 2,799,905.99

Questions 21-30.

DIRECTIONS: Each of Questions 21 through 30 consists of three lines of code letters and three lines of numbers. The numbers on each line should correspond with the code letters on the same line in accordance with the table below.

Code Letter	J	U	B	T	Y	D	K	R	L	P
Corresponding Number	0	1	2	3	4	5	5	7	8	9

On some of the lines, an error exists in the coding. Compare the letters and numbers in each question carefully. If you find an error or errors on:
only *one* of the lines in the question, mark your answer A;
any *two* lines in the question, mark your answer B;
all *three* lines in the question, mark your answer C;
none of the lines in the question, mark your answer D.

SAMPLE QUESTION

BJRPYUR   2079417
DTBPYKJ   5328460
YKLDBLT   4685283

In the above sample, the first line is correct since each code letter listed has the correct corresponding number. On the second line, an error exists because code letter P should have the number 9 instead of the number 8. The third line is correct since each code letter listed has the correct corresponding number. Since there is an error in *one* of the three lines, the correct answer is A. Now answer Questions 21 through 30 in the same manner.

21. BYPDTJL   2495308
    PLRDTJU   9815301
    DTJRYLK   5207486

22. RPBYRJK   7934706
    PKTYLBU   9624821
    KDLPJYR   6489047

5 (#2)

23. TPYBUJR   3942107   23._____
    BYRKPTU   2476931
    DUKPYDL   5169458

24. KBYDLPL   6345898   24._____
    BLRKBRU   2876261
    JTULDYB   0318542

25. LDPYDKR   8594567   25._____
    BDKDRJL   2565708
    BDRPLUJ   2679810

26. PLRLBPU   9858291   26._____
    LPYKRDJ   88936750
    TDKPDTR   3569527

27. RKURPBY   7617924   27._____
    RYUKPTJ   7426930
    RTKPTJD   7369305

28. DYKPBJT   5469203   28._____
    KLPJBTL   6890238
    TKPLBJP   3698209

29. BTPRJYL   2397148   29._____
    LDKUTYR   8561347
    YDBLRPJ   4528190

30. ULPBKYT   1892643   30._____
    KPDTRBJ   6953720
    YLKJPTB   4860932

KEY (CORRECT ANSWERS)

1.	A	11.	D	21.	B
2.	C	12.	C	22.	C
3.	A	13.	A	23.	D
4.	D	14.	B	24.	B
5.	C	15.	A	25.	A
6.	C	16.	B	26.	C
7.	C	17.	C	27.	A
8.	D	18.	B	28.	D
9.	A	19.	A	29.	B
10.	B	20.	B	30.	D

CLERICAL ABILITIES
EXAMINATION SECTION
TEST 1

DIRECTIONS: Each question or incomplete statement is followed by several suggested answers or completions. Select the one that BEST answers the question or completes the statement. *PRINT THE LETTER OF THE CORRECT ANSWER IN THE SPACE AT THE RIGHT.*

Questions 1-4.

DIRECTIONS: Questions 1 through 4 are to be answered on the basis of the information given below.

The most commonly used filing system and the one that is easiest to learn is alphabetical filing. This involves putting records in an A to Z order, according to the letters of the alphabet. The name of a person is filed by using the following order: first, the surname or last name; second, the first name; third, the middle name or middle initial. For example, *Henry C. Young* is filed under *Y* and thereafter under *Young, Henry C.* The name of a company is filed in the same way. For example, *Long Cabinet Co.* is filed under *L* while *John T. Long Cabinet Co.* is filed under *L* and thereafter under *Long, John T. Cabinet Co.*

1. The one of the following which lists the names of persons in the CORRECT alphabetical order is:
   A. Mary Carrie, Helen Carrol, James Carson, John Carter
   B. James Carson, Mary Carrie, John Carter, Helen Carrol
   C. Helen Carrol, James Carson, John Carter, Mary Carrie
   D. John Carter, Helen Carrol, Mary Carrie, James Carson

1.____

2. The one of the following which lists the names of persons in the CORRECT alphabetical order is:
   A. Jones, John C.; Jones, John A.; Jones, John P.; Jones, John K.
   B. Jones, John P.; Jones, John K.; Jones, John C.; Jones, John A.
   C. Jones, John A.; Jones, John C.; Jones, John K.; Jones, John P.
   D. Jones, John K.; Jones, John C.; Jones, John A.; Jones, John P.

2.____

3. The one of the following which lists the names of the companies in the CORRECT alphabetical order is:
   A. Blane Co., Blake Co., Block Co., Blear Co.
   B. Blake Co., Blane Co., Blear Co., Block Co.
   C. Block Co., Blear Co., Blane Co., Blake Co.
   D. Blear Co., Blake Co., Blane Co., Block Co.

3.____

4. You are to return to the file an index card on *Barry C. Wayne Materials and Supplies Co.*
Of the following, the CORRECT alphabetical group that you should return the index card to is
  A. A to G   B. H to M   C. N to S   D. T to Z

4.____

Questions 5-10.

DIRECTIONS: In each of Questions 5 through 10, the names of four people are given. For each question, choose as your answer the one of the four names given which should be filed FIRST according to the usual system of alphabetical filing of names, as described in the following paragraph.

In filing names, you must start with the last name. Names are filed in order of the first letter of the last name, then the second letter, etc. Therefore, BAILY would be filed before BROWN, which would be filed before COLT. A name with fewer letters of the same type comes first, i.e., Smith before Smithe. If the last names are the same, the names are filed alphabetically by the first name. If the first name is an initial, a name with an initial would come before a first name that starts with the same letter as the initial. Therefore, I. BROWN would come before IRA BROWN. Finally, if both last name and first name are the same, the name would be filed alphabetically by the middle name, once again an initial coming before a middle name which starts with the same letter as the initial. If there is no middle name at all, the name would come before those with middle initials or names.

SAMPLE QUESTION: A. Lester Daniels
                  B. William Dancer
                  C. Nathan Danzig
                  D. Dan Lester

The last names beginning with D are filed before the last name beginning with L. Since DANIELS, DANCER, and DANZIG all begin with the same three letters, you must look at the fourth letter of the last name to determine which name should be filed first. C comes before I or Z in the alphabet, so DANCER is filed before DANIELS or DANZIG. Therefore, the answer to the above sample question is B.

5. A. Scott Biala
    B. Mary Byala
    C. Martin Baylor
    D. Francis Bauer

5.____

6. A. Howard J. Black
    B. Howard Black
    C. J. Howard Black
    D. John H. Black

6.____

7. A. Theodora Garth Kingston
    B. Theadore Barth Kingston
    C. Thomas Kingston
    D. Thomas T. Kingston

7.____

8. A. Paulette Mary Huerta
    B. Paul M. Huerta
    C. Paulette L. Huerta
    D. Peter A. Huerta

9. A. Martha Hunt Morgan
    B. Martin Hunt Morgan
    C. Mary H. Morgan
    D. Martine H. Morgan

10. A. James T. Meerschaum
    B. James M. Mershum
    C. James F. Mearshaum
    D. James N. Meshum

Questions 11-14.

DIRECTIONS: Questions 11 through 14 are to be answered SOLELY on the basis of the following information.

You are required to file various documents in file drawers which are labeled according to the following pattern:

DOCUMENTS

MEMOS		LETTERS	
File	Subject	File	Subject
84PM1	(A-L)	84PC1	(A-L)
84PM2	(M-Z)	84PC2	(M-Z)

REPORTS		INQUIRIES	
File	Subject	File	Subject
84PR1	(A-L)	84PQ1	(A-L)
84PR2	(M-Z)	84PQ2	(M-Z)

11. A letter dealing with a burglary should be filed in the drawer labeled
    A. 84PM1   B. 84PC1   C. 84PR1   D. 84PQ2

12. A report on Statistics should be found in the drawer labeled
    A. 84PM1   B. 84PC2   C. 84PR2   D. 84PQS

13. An inquiry is received about parade permit procedures. It should be filed in the drawer labeled
    A. 84PM2   B. 84PC1   C. 84PR1   D. 84PQ2

14. A police officer has a question about a robbery report you filed. You should pull this file from the drawer labeled
    A. 84PM1   B. 84PM2   C. 84PR1   D. 84PR2

Questions 15-22.

DIRECTIONS: Each of Questions 15 through 22 consists of four or six numbered names. For each question, choose the option (A, B, C, or D) which indicates the order in which the names should be filed in accordance with the following filing instructions:
- File alphabetically according to last name, then first name, then middle initial.
- File according to each successive letter within a name.
- When comparing two names in which the letters in the longer name are identical to the corresponding letters in the shorter name, the shorter name is filed first.
- When the last names are the same, initials are always filed before names beginning with the same letter.

15.   I.   Ralph Robinson
      II. Alfred Ross
      III. Luis Robles
      IV. James Roberts

The CORRECT filing sequence for the above names should be
A. IV, II, I, III   B. I, IV, III, II   C. III, IV, I, II   D. IV, I, III, II

16.   I.   Irwin Goodwin
      II. Inez Gonzalez
      III. Irene Goodman
      IV. Ira S. Goodwin
      V.   Ruth I. Goldstein
      VI. M.B. Goodman

The CORRECT filing sequence for the above names should be
A. V, II, I, IV, III, VI
B. V, II, VI, III, IV, I
C. V, II, III, VI, IV, I
D. V, II, III, VI, I, IV

17.   I.   George Allan
      II. Gregory Allen
      III. Gary Allen
      IV. George Allen

The CORRECT filing sequence for the above names should be
A. IV, III, I, II   B. I, IV, II, III   C. III, IV, I, II   D. I, III, IV, II

5 (#1)

18. I. Simon Kauffman
     II. Leo Kaufman
     III. Robert Kaufmann
     IV. Paul Kauffmann

   The CORRECT filing sequence for the above names should be
   A. I, IV, II, III   B. II, IV, III, I   C. III, II, IV, I   D. I, II, III, IV

18.____

19. I. Roberta Williams
     II. Robin Wilson
     III. Roberta Wilson
     IV. Robin Williams

   The CORRECT filing sequence for the above names should be
   A. III, II, IV, I   B. I, IV, III, II   C. I, II, III, IV   D. III, I, II, IV

19.____

20. I. Lawrence Shultz
     II. Albert Schultz
     III. Theodore Schwartz
     IV. Thomas Schwarz
     V. Alvin Schultz
     VI. Leonard Shultz

   The CORRECT filing sequence for the above names should be
   A. II, V, III, IV, I, VI   B. IV, III, V, I, II, VI
   C. II, V, I, VI, III, IV   D. I, VI, II, V, III, IV

20.____

21. I. McArdle
     II. Mayer
     III. Maletz
     IV. McNiff
     V. Meyer
     VI. MacMahon

   The CORRECT filing sequence for the above names should be
   A. I, IV, VI, III, II, V   B. II, I, IV, VI, III, V
   C. VI, III, II, I, IV, V   D. VI, III, II, V, I, IV

21.____

22. I. Jack E. Johnson
     II. R.H. Jackson
     III. Bertha Jackson
     IV. J.T. Johnson
     V. Ann Johns
     VI. John Jacobs

   The CORRECT filing sequence for the above names should be
   A. II, III, VI, V, IV, I   B. III, II, VI, V, IV, I
   C. VI, II, III, I, V, IV   D. III, II, VI, IV, V, I

22.____

Questions 23-30.

DIRECTIONS: The code table below shows 10 letters with matching numbers. For each question, there are three sets of letters. Each set of letters is followed by a set of numbers which may or may not match their correct letter according to the code table. For each question, check all three sets of letters and numbers and mark your answer:
    A. if no pairs are correctly matched
    B. if only one pair is correctly matched
    C. if only two pairs are correctly matched
    D. if all three pairs are correctly matched

CODE TABLE

T	M	V	D	S	P	R	G	B	H
1	2	3	4	5	6	7	8	9	0

SAMPLE QUESTION: TMVDSP – 123456
                                 RGBHTM – 789011
                                 DSPRGB – 256789

In the sample question above, the first set of numbers correctly match its set of letters. But the second and third pairs contain mistakes. In the second pair, M is correctly matched with number 1. According to the code table, letter M should be correctly matched with number 2. In the third pair, the letter D is incorrectly matched with number 2. According to the code table, letter D should be correctly matched with number 4. Since only one of the pairs is correctly matched, the answer to this sample question is B.

23.   RSBMRM – 759262
        GDSRVH – 845730
        VDBRTM - 349713

24.   TGVSDR – 183247
        SMHRDP – 520647
        TRMHSR - 172057

25.   DSPRGM – 456782
        MVDBHT – 234902
        HPMDBT - 062491

26.   BVPTRD – 936184
        GDPHMB – 807029
        GMRHMV - 827032

27.   MGVRSH – 283750
        TRDMBS – 174295
        SPRMGV - 567283

23.____

24.____

25.____

26.____

27.____

28. SGBSDM – 489542   28.____
    MGHPTM – 290612
    MPBMHT - 269301

29. TDPBHM – 146902   29.____
    VPBMRS – 369275
    GDMBHM - 842902

30. MVPTBV – 236194   30.____
    PDRTMB – 47128
    BGTMSM - 981232

KEY (CORRECT ANSWERS)

1. A	11. B	21. C
2. C	12. C	22. B
3. B	13. D	23. B
4. D	14. D	24. B
5. D	15. D	25. C
6. B	16. C	26. A
7. B	17. D	27. D
8. B	18. A	28. A
9. A	19. B	29. D
10. C	20. A	30. A

TEST 2

DIRECTIONS: Each question or incomplete statement is followed by several suggested answers or completions. Select the one that BEST answers the question or completes the statement. *PRINT THE LETTER OF THE CORRECT ANSWER IN THE SPACE AT THE RIGHT.*

Questions 1-10.

DIRECTIONS: Questions 1 through 10 each consists of two columns, each containing four lines of names, numbers and/or addresses. For each question, compare the lines in Column I with the lines in Column II to see if they match exactly, and mark your answer A, B, C, or D, according to the following instructions:
    A. all four lines match exactly
    B. only three lines match exactly
    C. only two lines match exactly
    D. only one line matches exactly

    COLUMN I   COLUMN II

1.   I.   Earl Hodgson   Earl Hodgson   1.____
     II.   1409870   1408970
     III.   Shore Ave.   Schore Ave.
     IV.   Macon Rd.   Macon Rd.

2.   I.   9671485   9671485   2.____
     II.   470 Astor Court   470 Astor Court
     III.   Halprin, Phillip   Halperin, Phillip
     IV.   Frank D. Poliseo   Frank D. Poliseo

3.   I.   Tandem Associates   Tandom Associates   3.____
     II.   144-17 Northern Blvd.   144-17 Northern Blvd.
     III.   Alberta Forchi   Albert Forchi
     IV.   Kings Park, NY 10751   Kings Point, NY 10751

4.   I.   Bertha C. McCormack   Bertha C. McCormack   4.____
     II.   Clayton, MO   Clayton, MO
     III.   976-4242   976-4242
     IV.   New City, NY 10951   New City, NY 10951

5.   I.   George C. Morill   George C. Morrill   5.____
     II.   Columbia, SC 29201   Columbia, SD 29201
     III.   Louis Ingham   Louis Ingham
     IV.   3406 Forest Ave.   3406 Forest Ave.

6.   I.   506 S. Elliott Pl.   506 S. Elliott Pl.   6.____
     II.   Herbert Hall   Hurbert Hall
     III.   4712 Rockaway Pkway   4712 Rockaway Pkway
     IV.   169 E. 7 St.   169 E. 7 St.

7.
I. 345 Park Ave.
II. Colman Oven Corp.
III. Robert Conte
IV. 6179846

345 Park Pl.
Coleman Oven Corp.
Robert Conti
6179846

7._____

8.
I. Grigori Schierber
II. Des Moines, Iowa
III. Gouverneur Hospital
IV. 91-35 Cresskill Pl.

Grigori Schierber
Des Moines, Iowa
Gouverneur Hospital
91-35 Cresskill Pl.

8._____

9.
I. Jeffery Janssen
II. 8041071
III. 40 Rockefeller Plaza
IV. 407 6 St.

Jeffrey Janssen
8041071
40 Rockafeller Plaza
406 7 St.

9._____

10.
I. 5971996
II. 3113 Knickerbocker Ave.
III. 8434 Boston Post Rd.
IV. Penn Station

5871996
31123 Knickerbocker Ave.
8424 Boston Post Rd.
Penn Station

10._____

Questions 11-14.

DIRECTIONS: Questions 11 through 14 are to be answered by looking at the four groups of names and addresses listed below (I, II, III, and IV), and then finding out the number of groups that have their corresponding numbered lies exactly the same.

GROUP I
Line 1. Richmond General Hospital
Line 2. Geriatric Clinic
Line 3. 3975 Paerdegat St.
Line 4. Loudonville, New York 11538

GROUP II
Richman General Hospital
Geriatric Clinic
3975 Peardegat St.
Londonville, New York 11538

GROUP III
Line 1. Richmond General Hospital
Line 2. Geriatric Clinic
Line 3. 3795 Paerdegat St.
Line 4. Loudonville, New York 11358

GROUP IV
Richmend General Hospital
Geriatric Clinic
3975 Paerdegat St.
Loudonville, New York 11538

1. In how many groups is line one exactly the same?
   A. Two   B. Three   C. Four   D. None

11._____

12. In how many groups is line two exactly the same?
   A. Two   B. Three   C. Four   D. None

12._____

13. In how many groups is line three exactly the same?
   A. Two   B. Three   C. Four   D. None

13._____

14. In how many groups is line four exactly the same? 14._____
    A. Two   B. Three   C. Four   D. None

Questions 15-18.

DIRECTIONS: Each of Questions 15 through 18 has two lists of names and addresses. Each list contains three sets of names and addresses. Check each of the three sets in the list on the right to see if they are the same as the corresponding set in the list on the left. Mark your answers:
   A. if none of the sets in the right list are the same as those in the left list
   B. if only one of the sets in the right list is the same as those in the left list
   C. if only two of the sets in the right list are the same as those in the left list
   D. if all three sets in the right list are the same as those in the left list

15. Mary T. Berlinger   Mary T. Berlinger   15._____
    2351 Hampton St.   2351 Hampton St.
    Monsey, N.Y. 20117   Monsey, N.Y. 20117

    Eduardo Benes   Eduardo Benes
    483 Kingston Avenue   473 Kingston Avenue
    Central Islip, N.Y. 11734   Central Islip, N.Y. 11734

    Alan Carrington Fuchs   Alan Carrington Fuchs
    17 Gnarled Hollow Road   17 Gnarled Hollow Road
    Los Angeles, CA 91635   Los Angeles, CA 91685

16. David John Jacobson   David John Jacobson   16._____
    178 34 St. Apt. 4C   178 53 St. Apt. 4C
    New York, N.Y. 00927   New York, N.Y. 00927

    Ann-Marie Calonella   Ann-Marie Calonella
    7243 South Ridge Blvd.   7243 South Ridge Blvd.
    Bakersfield, CA 96714   Bakersfield, CA 96714

    Pauline M. Thompson   Pauline M. Thomson
    872 Linden Ave.   872 Linden Ave.
    Houston, Texas 70321   Houston, Texas 70321

17. Chester LeRoy Masterton   Chester LeRoy Masterson   17._____
    152 Lacy Rd.   152 Lacy Rd.
    Kankakee, Ill. 54532   Kankakee, Ill. 54532

    William Maloney   William Maloney
    S. LaCrosse Pla.   S. LaCross Pla.
    Wausau, Wisconsin 52136   Wausau, Wisconsin 52146

    Cynthia V. Barnes   Cynthia V. Barnes
    16 Pines Rd.   16 Pines Rd.
    Greenpoint, Miss. 20376   Greenpoint,, Miss. 20376

18. Marcel Jean Frontenac   Marcel Jean Frontenac   18._____
    8 Burton On The Water   6 Burton On The Water
    Calender, Me. 01471   Calender, Me. 01471

    J. Scott Marsden   J. Scott Marsden
    174 S. Tipton St.   174 Tipton St.
    Cleveland, Ohio   Cleveland, Ohio

    Lawrence T. Haney   Lawrence T. Haney
    171 McDonough St.   171 McDonough St.
    Decatur, Ga. 31304   Decatur, Ga. 31304

Questions 19-26.

DIRECTIONS: Each of Questions 19 through 26 has two lists of numbers. Each list contains three sets of numbers. Check each of the three sets in the list on the right to see if they are the same as the corresponding set in the list on the left. Mark your answers:
- A. if none of the sets in the right list are the same as those in the left list
- B. if only one of the sets in the right list is the same as those in the left list
- C. if only two of the sets in the right list are the same as those in the left list
- D. if all three sets in the right list are the same as those in the left lists

19. 7354183476   7354983476   19._____
    4474747744   4474747774
    5791430231   57914302311

20. 7143592185   7143892185   20._____
    8344517699   8344518699
    9178531263   9178531263

21. 2572114731   257214731   21._____
    8806835476   8806835476
    8255831246   8255831246

22. 331476853821   331476858621   22._____
    6976658532996   6976655832996
    3766042113715   3766042113745

23. 8806663315   88066633115   23._____
    74477138449   74477138449
    211756663666   211756663666

109

24. 990006966996   99000696996   24._____
    53022219743   53022219843
    4171171117717   4171171177717

25. 24400222433004   24400222433004   25._____
    5300030055000355   5300030055500355
    20000075532002022   20000075532002022

26. 6111666406600011116   61116664066001116   26._____
    7111300117001100733   7111300117001100733
    26666446664476518   26666446664476518

Questions 27-30.

DIRECTIONS: Questions 27 through 30 are to be answered by picking the answer which is in the correct numerical order, from the lowest number to the highest number, in each question.

27. A. 44533, 44518, 44516, 44547   27._____
    B. 44516, 44518, 44533, 44547
    C. 44547, 44533, 44518, 44516
    D. 44518, 44516, 44547, 44533

28. A. 95587, 95593, 95601, 95620   28._____
    B. 95601, 95620, 95587, 95593
    C. 95593, 95587, 95601. 95620
    D. 95620, 95601, 95593, 95587

29. A. 232212, 232208, 232232, 232223   29._____
    B. 232208, 232223, 232212, 232232
    C. 232208, 232212, 232223, 232232
    D. 232223, 232232, 232208, 232208

30. A. 113419, 113521, 113462, 113462   30._____
    B. 113588, 113462, 113521, 113419
    C. 113521, 113588, 113419, 113462
    D. 113419, 113462, 113521, 113588

KEY (CORRECT ANSWERS)

1.	C	11.	A	21.	C
2.	B	12.	C	22.	A
3.	D	13.	A	23.	D
4.	A	14.	A	24.	A
5.	C	15.	C	25.	C
6.	B	16.	B	26.	C
7.	D	17.	B	27.	B
8.	A	18.	B	28.	A
9.	D	19.	B	29.	C
10.	C	20.	B	30.	D

CODING

COMMENTARY

An ingenious question-type called coding, involving elements of alphabetizing, filing, name and number comparison, and evaluative judgment and application, has currently won wide acceptance in testing circles for measuring clerical aptitude and general ability, particularly on the senior (middle) grades (levels).

While the directions for this question-type usually vary in detail, the candidate is generally asked to consider groups of names, codes, and numbers, and, then, according to a given plan, to arrange codes in alphabetic order; to arrange these in numerical sequence; to re-arrange columns of names and numbers in correct order; to espy errors in coding; to choose the correct coding arrangement in consonance with the given directions and examples, etc.

This question-type appears to have few parameters in respect to form, substance, or degree of difficulty.

Accordingly, acquaintance with, and practice in the coding question is recommended for the serious candidate.

EXAMINATION SECTION
TEST 1

DIRECTIONS: Questions 1 through 10 are to be answered on the basis of the following Code Table. In this table every letter has a corresponding code number to be punched. Each question contains three lines of letters and code numbers. In each line, the code numbers should correspond with the letters in accordance with the table.

Letter	M	X	R	T	W	A	E	Q	Z	C
Code	1	2	3	4	5	6	7	8	9	0

On some of the lines, an error exists in the coding. Compare the letters and numbers in each question carefully. If you find an error or errors on
    only *one* of the lines in the question, mark your answer A;
    any *two* lines in the question, mark your answer B;
    all *three* lines in the question, mark your answer C;
    none of the lines in the question, mark your answer D.

SAMPLE QUESTION

XAQMZMRQ	-	26819138
RAERQEX	-	3573872
TMZCMTZA	-	46901496

In the above sample, the first line is correct since each letter, as listed, has the correct corresponding code number.
In the second line, an error exists because the letter A should have the code number 6 instead of 5.
In the third line, an error exists because the letter W should have the code number 5 instead of 6.
Since there are errors in two of the three lines, your answer should be B.

1. EQRMATTR   -   78316443
    MACWXRQW   -   16052385
    XZEMCAR   -   2971063

2. CZEMRXQ   -   0971238
    XMTARET   -   2146374
    WCEARWEC   -   50863570

3. CEXAWRQZ   -   07265389
    RCRMMZQT   -   33011984
    ACMZWTEX   -   60195472

4. XRCZQZWR   -   23089953
    CMRQCAET   -   01389574
    ZXRWTECM   -   92345701

2 (#1)

5.	AXMTRAWR	-	62134653		5.___
	EQQCZCEW	-	77809075		
	MAZQARTM	-	16086341		
6.	WRWQCTRM	-	53580431		6.___
	CXMWAERZ	-	02156739		
	RCQEWWME	-	30865517		
7.	CRMECEAX	-	03170762		7.___
	MZCTRXRQ	-	19043238		
	XXZREMEW	-	22937175		
8.	MRCXQEAX	-	13928762		8.___
	WAMZTRMZ	-	65194319		
	ECXARWXC	-	70263520		
9.	MAWXECRQ	-	16527038		9.___
	RXQEAETM	-	32876741		
	RXEWMCZQ	-	32751098		
10.	MRQZCATE	-	13890647		10.___
	WCETRXAW	-	50743625		
	CZWMCERT	-	09510734		

KEY (CORRECT ANSWERS)

1. D
2. B
3. A
4. C
5. C

6. A
7. D
8. B
9. D
10. A

TEST 2

DIRECTIONS: Questions 1 through 6 consist of three lines of code letters and numbers. The numbers on each line should correspond with the code letters on the same line in accordance with the table below.

Code Letter	F	X	L	M	R	W	T	S	B	H
Corresponding Number	0	1	2	3	4	5	6	7	8	9

On some of the lines, an error exists in the coding. Compare the letters and numbers in each question carefully. If you find an error or errors on
    only *one* of the lines in the question, mark your answer A;
    any *two* lines in the question, mark your answer B;
    all *three* lines in the question, mark your answer C;
    none of the lines in the question, mark your answer D.

SAMPLE QUESTION

    LTSXHMF   2671930
    TBRWHLM   6845913
    SXLBFMR   5128034

In the above sample, the first line is correct since each code letter listed has the correct corresponding number.
    On the second line, an error exists because code letter L should have the number 2 instead of the number 1.
    On the third line, an error exists because the code letter S should have the number 7 instead of the number 5.
    Since there are errors on two of the three lines, the correct answer is B.

1.   XMWBHLR   1358924   1.____
    FWSLRHX   0572491
    MTXBLTS   3618267

2.   XTLSMRF   1627340   2.____
    BMHRFLT   8394026
    HLTSWRX   9267451

3.   LMBSFXS   2387016   3.____
    RWLMBSX   4532871
    SMFXBHW   7301894

4.   RSTWTSML   47657632   4.____
    LXRMHFBS   21439087
    FTLBMRWX   06273451

5.   XSRSBWFM   17478603   5.____
    BRMXRMXT   84314216
    XSTFBWRL   17609542

6. TMSBXHLS   63781927
    RBSFLFWM   48702053
    MHFXWTRS   39015647

6.___

KEY (CORRECT ANSWERS)

1. D
2. A
3. C
4. B
5. C
6. D

TEST 3

DIRECTIONS: Questions 1 through 5 consist of three lines of code letters and numbers. The numbers on each line should correspond with the code letters on the same line in accordance with the table below.

Code Letter	P	L	I	J	B	O	H	U	C	G
Corresponding Number	0	1	2	3	4	5	6	7	8	9

On some of the lines, an error exists in the coding. Compare the letters and numbers in each question carefully. If you find an error or errors on
   only *one* of the lines in the question, mark your answer A;
   any *two* lines in the question, mark your answer B;
   all *three* lines in the question, mark your answer C;
   none of the lines in the question, mark your answer D.

SAMPLE QUESTION

JHOILCP	3652180
BICLGUP	4286970
UCIBHLJ	5824613

In the above sample, the first line is correct since each code letter listed has the correct corresponding number.
On the second line, an error exists because code letter L should have the number 1 instead of the number 6.
On the third line an error exists because the code letter U should have the number 7 instead of the number 5.
Since there are errors on two of the three lines, the correct answer is B.

1. BULJCIP 4713920
   HIGPOUL 6290571
   OCUHJBI 5876342

2. CUBLOIJ 8741023
   LCLGCLB 1818914
   JPUHIOC 3076158

3. OIJGCBPO 52398405
   UHPBLIOP 76041250
   CLUIPGPC 81720908

4. BPCOUOJI 40875732
   UOHCIPLB 75682014
   GLHUUCBJ 92677843

5. HOIOHJLH 65256361
   IOJJHHBP 25536640
   OJHBJOPI 53642502

1. ____
2. ____
3. ____
4. ____
5. ____

119

KEY (CORRECT ANSWERS)

1. A
2. C
3. D
4. B
5. C

TEST 4

DIRECTIONS: Questions 1 through 5 consist of three lines of code letters and numbers. The numbers on each line should correspond with the code letters on the same line in accordance with the table below.

Code Letters	Q	S	L	Y	M	O	U	N	W	Z
Corresponding Numbers	1	2	3	4	5	6	7	8	9	0

On some of the lines, an error exists in the coding. Compare the letters and numbers in each question carefully. If you find an error on

only *one* of the lines in the question, mark your answer A;
any *two* lines in the question, mark your answer B;
all *three* lines in the question, mark your answer C;
none of the lines in the question, mark your answer D.

SAMPLE QUESTION
MOQNWZQS   56189012
QWNMOLYU   19865347
LONLMYWN   36835489

In the above sample, the first line is correct since each code letter, as listed, has the correct corresponding number.
On the second line, an error exists because code letter M should have the number 5 instead of the number 6.
On the third line an error exists because the code letter W should have the number 9 instead of the number 8.
Since there are errors on two of the three lines, the correct answer is B.

1. SMUWOLQN   25796318
    ULSQNMZL   73218503
    NMYQZUSL   85410723   1._____

2. YUWWMYQZ   47995410
    SOSOSQSO   26262126
    ZUNLWMYW   07839549   2._____

3. QULSWZYN   17329045
    ZYLQWOYF   04319639
    QLUYWZSO   13749026   3._____

4. NLQZOYUM   83106475
    SQMUWZOM   21579065
    MMYWMZSQ   55498021   4._____

5. NQLOWZZU   81319007
    SMYLUNZO   25347806
    UWMSNZOL   79528013   5._____

KEY (CORRECT ANSWERS)

1. D
2. D
3. B
4. A
5. C

TEST 5

DIRECTIONS: Answer Questions 1 through 6 SOLELY on the basis of the chart and the instructions given below.

Toll Rate	$.25	$.30	$.45	$.60	$.75	$8.90	$1.20	$2.50
Classification Number of Vehicle	1	2	3	4	5	6	7	8

Assume that each of the amounts of money on the above chart is a toll rate charged for a type of vehicle and that the number immediately below each amount is the classification number for that type of vehicle. For instance, "1" is the classification number for a vehicle paying a $.25 toll; "2" is the classification number for a vehicle paying a $.30 toll; and so forth.

In each question, a series of tolls is given in Column I. Column II gives four different arrangements of classification numbers. You are to pick the answer (A, B, C, or D) in Column II that gives the classification numbers that match the tolls in Column I and are in the same order as the tolls in Column I.

SAMPLE QUESTION

Column I
$.30, $.90, $2.50, $.45

Column II
A. 2, 6, 8, 2
B. 2, 8, 6, 3
C. 2, 6, 8, 3
D. 1, 6, 8, 3

According to the chart, the classification numbers that correspond to these toll rates are as follows: $.30 - 2, $.90 - 6, $2.50 - 8, $.45 - 3. Therefore, the right answer is 2, 6, 8, 3. The answer is C in Column II.

Do the following questions in the same way.

Column I

1. $.60, $.30, $.90, $1.20, $.60

2. $.90, $.45, $.25, $.45, $2.50, $.75

3. $.45, $.75, $1.20, $.25, $.25, $.30, $.45

4. $1.20, $2.50, $.45, $.90, $1.20, $.75, $.25

Column II

1. A. 4, 6, 2, 8, 4
    B. 4, 2, 6, 7, 4
    C. 2, 4, 7, 6, 2
    D. 2, 4, 6, 7, 4

2. A. 6, 3, 1, 3, 8, 3
    B. 6, 3, 3, 1, 8, 5
    C. 6, 1, 3, 3, 8, 5
    D. 6, 3, 1, 3, 8, 5

3. A. 3, 5, 7, 1, 1, 2, 3
    B. 5, 3, 7, 1, 1, 2, 3
    C. 3, 5, 7, 1, 2, 1, 3
    D. 3, 7, 5, 1, 1, 2, 3

4. A. 7, 8, 5, 6, 7, 5, 1
    B. 7, 8, 3, 7, 6, 5, 1
    C. 7, 8, 3, 6, 7, 5, 1
    D. 7, 8, 3, 6, 7, 1, 5

1._____

2._____

3._____

4._____

2 (#5)

5. $2.50, $1.20, $.90, $.25, $.60, $.45, $.30
    A. 8, 6, 7, 1, 4, 3, 2
    B. 8, 7, 5, 1, 4, 3, 2
    C. 8, 7, 6, 2, 4, 3, 2
    D. 8, 7, 6, 1, 4, 3, 2

5. __

6. $.75, $.25, $.45, $.60, $.90, $.30, $2.50
    A. 5, 1, 3, 2, 4, 6, 8
    B. 5, 1, 3, 4, 2, 6, 8
    C. 5, 1, 3, 4, 6, 2, 8
    D. 5, 3, 1, 4, 6, 2, 8

6. __

KEY (CORRECT ANSWERS)

1. B
2. D
3. A
4. C
5. D
6. C

TEST 6

DIRECTIONS: Answer Questions 1 through 10 on the basis of the following information:
A code number for any item is obtained by combining the date of delivery, number of units received, and number of units used. The first two digits represent the day of the month, the third and fourth digits represent the month, and the fifth and sixth digits represent the year.
The number following the letter R represents the number of units received and the number following the letter U represents the number of units used.
For example, the code number 120603-R5690-U1001 indicates that a delivery of 5,690 units was made on June 12, 2003 of which 1,001 units were used.

Questions 1-6.

DIRECTIONS: Using the chart below, answer Questions 1 through 6 by choosing the letter (A, B, C, or D) in which the supplier and stock number correspond to the code number given.

Supplier	Stock Number	Number of Units Received	Delivery Date	Number of Units Used
Stony	38390	8300	May 11, 2002	3800
Stoney	39803	1780	September 15, 2003	1703
Nievo	21220	5527	October 10, 2003	5007
Nieve	38903	1733	August 5, 2003	1703
Monte	39213	5527	October 10, 2002	5007
Stony	38890	3308	December 9, 2002	3300
Stony	83930	3880	September 12, 2002	380
Nevo	47101	485	June 11, 2002	231
Nievo	12122	5725	May 11, 2003	5201
Neve	47101	9721	August 15, 2003	8207
Nievo	21120	2275	January 7, 2002	2175
Rosa	41210	3821	March 3, 2003	2710
Stony	38890	3308	September 12, 2002	3300
Dinal	54921	1711	April 2, 2003	1117
Stony	33890	8038	March 5, 2003	3300
Dinal	54721	1171	March 2, 2002	717
Claridge	81927	3308	April 5, 2003	3088
Nievo	21122	4878	June 7, 2002	3492
Haley	39670	8300	December 23, 2003	5300

1. Code No. 120902-R3308-U3300   1._____

   A. Nievo - 12122   B. Stony - 83930
   C. Nievo - 21220   D. Stony -38890

2. Code No. 101002-R5527-U5007   2._____

   A. Nievo - 21220   B. Haley - 39670
   C. Monte - 39213   D. Claridge - 81927

3. Code No. 101003-R5527-U5007   3._____

   A. Nievo - 21220   B. Monte - 39213
   C. Nievo - 12122   D. Nievo - 21120

125

2 (#6)

4. Code No. 110503-R5725-U5201

    A. Nievo - 12122   B. Nievo - 21220
    C. Haley - 39670   D. Stony - 38390

4.___

5. Code No. 070102-R2275-U2175

    A. Stony - 33890   B. Stony - 83930
    C. Stony - 38390   D. Nievo - 21120

5.___

6. Code No. 120902-R3880-U380

    A. Stony - 83930   B. Stony - 38890
    C. Stony - 33890   D. Monte - 39213

6.___

Questions 7-10.

DIRECTIONS: Using the same chart, answer Questions 7 through 10 by choosing the letter (A, B, C, or D) in which the code number corresponds to the supplier and stock number given.

7. Nieve - 38903

    A. 851903-R1733-U1703   B. 080502-R1733-U1703
    C. 080503-R1733-U1703   D. 050803-R1733-U1703

7.___

8. Nevo - 47101

    A. 081503-R9721-U8207   B. 091503-R9721-U8207
    C. 110602-R485-U231   D. 061102-R485-U231

8.___

9. Dinal - 54921

    A. 020403-R1711-U1117   B. 030202-R1171-U717
    C. 020302-R1171-U717   D. 421903-R1711-U1117

9.___

10. Nievo - 21122

    A. 070602-R4878-U3492   B. 060702-R4878-U349
    C. 761902-R4878-U3492   D. 060702-R4878-U3492

10.___

KEY (CORRECT ANSWERS)

1. D
2. C
3. A
4. A
5. D

6. A
7. D
8. C
9. A
10. A

NAME AND NUMBER CHECKING
EXAMINATION SECTION
TEST 1

DIRECTIONS: Questions 1 through 17 consist of sets of names and addresses. In each question, the name and address in Column II should be an exact copy of the name and address in Column I.
If there is:
a mistake only in the name, mark your answer A;
a mistake only in the address, mark your answer B;
a mistake in both name and address, mark your answer C;
No mistake in either name or address, mark your answer D.

Sample Question

Column I
Christina Magnusson
288 Greene Street
New York, N.Y. 10003

Column II
Christina Magnusson
288 Greene Street
New York, N.Y. 10013

Since there is a mistake only in the address (the zip code should be 10003 instead of 10013), the answer to the sample question is B.

COLUMN I

1. Ms. Joan Kelly
   313 Franklin Avenue
   Brooklyn, N.Y. 11202

2. Mrs. Eileen Engel
   47-24 86 Road
   Queens, N.Y. 11122

3. Marcia Michaels
   213 E. 81 St.
   New York, N.Y. 10012

4. Rev. Edward J. Smyth
   1401 Brandeis Street
   San Francisco, Calif. 96201

5. Alicia Rodriguez
   24-68 82 St.
   Elmhurst, N.Y. 11122

COLUMN II

1. Ms. Joan Kielly
   318 Franklin Ave.
   Brooklyn, N.Y. 11202

2. Mrs. Ellen Engel
   47-24 86 Road
   Queens, New York 11122

3. Marcia Michaels
   213 E. 81 St.
   New York, N.Y. 10012

4. Rev. Edward J. Smyth
   1401 Brandies Street
   San Francisco, Calif. 96201

5. Alicia Rodriguez
   2468 81 St.
   Elmhurst, N.Y. 11122

1.____

2.____

3.____

4.____

5.____

2 (#1)

COLUMN I	COLUMN II	
6. Ernest Eisemann 21 Columbia St. New York, N.Y. 10007	Ernest Eisermann 21 Columbia St. New York, N.Y. 10007	6.____
7. Mr. & Mrs. George Petersson 87-11 91st Avenue Woodhaven, N.Y. 11421	Mr. & Mrs. George Peterson 87-11 91st Avenue Woodhaven, N.Y. 11421	7.____
8. Mr. Ivan Klebnikov 1848 Newkirk Avenue Brooklyn, N.Y. 11226	Mr. Ivan Klebikov 1848 Newkirk Avenue Brooklyn, N.Y. 11622	8.____
9. Mr. Samuel Rothfleisch 71 Pine Street New York, N.Y. 10005	Samuel Rothfleisch 71 Pine Street New York, N.Y. 100005	9.____
10. Mrs. Isabel Tonnessen 198 East 185th Street Bronx, N.Y. 10458	Mrs. Isabel Tonnessen 189 East 185th Street Bronx, N.Y. 10348	10.____
11. Esteban Perez 173 Eighth Street Staten Island, N.Y. 10306	Estaban Perez 173 Eighth Street Staten Island, N.Y. 10306	11.____
12. Esta Wong 141 West 68 St. New York, N.Y. 10023	Esta Wang 141 West 68 St. New York, N.Y. 10023	12.____
13. Dr. Alberto Grosso 3475 12th Avenue Brooklyn, N.Y. 11218	Dr. Alberto Grosso 3475 12th Avenue Brooklyn, N.Y. 11218	13.____
14. Mrs. Ruth Bortias 482 Theresa Ct. Far Rockaway, N.Y. 11691	Ms. Ruth Bortlas 482 Theresa Ct. Far Rockaway, N.Y. 11169	14.____
15. Mr. & Mrs. Howard Fox 2301 Sedgwick Ave. Bronx, N.Y. 10468	Mr. & Mrs. Howard Fox 231 Sedgwick Ave. Bronx, N.Y. 10468	15.____
16. Miss Marjorie Black 223 East 23 Street New York, N.Y. 10010	Miss Margorie Black 223 East 23 Street New York, N.Y. 10010	16.____

3 (#1)

COLUMN I	COLUMN II	
17. Michelle Herman 806 Valley Rd. Old Tappan, N.J. 07675	Michelle Hermann 806 Valley Dr. Old Tappan, N.J. 07675	17.____

KEY (CORRECT ANSWERS)

1.	C	7.	A	13.	D
2.	A	8.	C	14.	C
3.	D	9.	D	15.	B
4.	B	10.	B	16.	A
5.	B	11.	A	17.	C
6.	A	12.	D		

TEST 2

DIRECTIONS: Questions 1 through 15 are to be answered SOLELY on the instructions given below. *PRINT THE LETTER OF THE CORRECT ANSWER IN THE SPACE AT THE RIGHT.*

INSTRUCTIONS

In each of the following questions, the 3-line name and address in Column I is the master-list entry, and the 3-line entry in Column II is the information to be checked against the master list. If there is one line that does not match, mark your answer A; if there are two lines that do not match, mark your answer B; if all three lines do not match, mark your answer C; if the lines all match exactly, mark your answer D.

Sample Question

Column I
Mark L. Field
11-09 Price Park Blvd.
Bronx, N.Y. 11402

Column II
Mark L. Field
11-99 Prince Park Way
Bronx, N.Y. 11401

The first lines in each column match exactly. The second lines do not match since 11-09 does not match 11-99; and Blvd. does not match Way. The third lines do not match either since 11402 does not match 11401. Therefore, there are two lines that do not match, and the CORRECT answer is B.

COLUMN I

1. Jerome A. Jackson
   1243 14th Avenue
   New York, N.Y. 10023

2. Sophie Strachtheim
   33-28 Connecticut Ave.
   Far Rockaway, N.Y. 11697

3. Elisabeth N.T. Gorrell
   256 Exchange St.
   New York, N.Y. 10013

4. Maria J. Gonzalez
   7516 E. Sheepshead Rd.
   Brooklyn, N.Y. 11240

5. Leslie B. Brautenweiler
   21 57A Seiler Terr.
   Flushing, N.Y. 11367

COLUMN II

1. Jerome A. Johnson
   1234 14th Avenue
   New York, N.Y. 10023

2. Sophie Strachtheim
   33-28 Connecticut Ave.
   Far Rockaway, N.Y. 11697

3. Elizabeth N.T. Gorrell
   256 Exchange St.
   New York, N.Y. 10013

4. Maria J. Gonzalez
   7516 N. Shepshead Rd.
   Brooklyn, N.Y. 11240

5. Leslie B. Brautenwieler
   21-75A Seiler Terr.
   Flushing, N.J. 11367

2 (#2)

COLUMN I	COLUMN II	
6. Rigoberto J. Peredes 157 Twin Towers, #18F Tottenville, S. I., N.Y,	Rigoberto J. Peredes 157 Twin Towers, #18F Tottenville, S.I., N.Y.	6.____
7. Pietro F. Albino P.O. Box 7548 Floral Park, N.Y. 11005	Pietro F. Albina P.O. Box 7458 Floral Park, N.Y. 11005	7.____
8. Joanne Zimmerman Bldg. SW, Room 314 532-4601	Joanne Zimmermann Bldg. SW, Room 314 532-4601	8.____
9. Carlyle Whetstone Payroll Div. –A, Room 212A 262-5000, ext. 471	Carlyle Whetstone Payroll Div. –A, Room 212A 262-5000, ext. 417	9.____
10. Kenneth Chiang Legal Council, Room 9745 (201) 416-9100, ext. 17	Kenneth Chiang Legal Counsel, Room 9745 (201) 416-9100, Ext. 17	10.____
11. Ethel Koenig Personnel Services Division, Room 433; 635-7572	Ethel Hoenig Personal Services Division, Room 433; 635-7527	11.____
12. Joyce Ehrhardt Office of the Administrator, Room W56; 387-8706	Joyce Ehrhart Office of the Administrator, Room W56; 387-7806	12.____
13. Ruth Lang EAM Bldg., Room C101 625-2000, ext. 765	Ruth Lang EAM Bldg., Room C110 625-2000, ext. 765	13.____
14. Anne Marie Ionozzi Investigations, Room 827 576-4000, ext. 832	Anna Marie Ionozzi Investigation, Room 827 566-4000, ext. 832	14.____
15. Willard Jameson Fm C Bldg., Room 687 454-3010	Willard Jamieson Fm C Bldg., Room 687 454-3010	15.____

KEY (CORRECT ANSWERS)

1.	B	6.	D	C	C
2.	D	7.	B	12.	B
3.	A	8.	D	13.	A
4.	A	9.	B	14.	C
5.	C	10.	A	15.	A

TEST 3

DIRECTIONS: Questions 1 through 10 are to be answered on the basis of the following instructions. *PRINT THE LETTER OF THE CORRECT ANSWER IN THE SPACE AT THE RIGHT.*

INSTRUCTIONS

For each such set of names, addresses, and numbers listed in Columns I and II, select your answer from the following options:
The names in Columns I and II are different,
The addresses in Columns I and II are different,
The numbers in Columns I and II are different,
The names, addresses, and numbers in Columns I and II are identical.

	COLUMN I	COLUMN II	
1.	Francis Jones 62 Stately Avenue 96-12446	Francis Jones 62 Stately Avenue 96-21446	1.____
2.	Julio Montez 19 Ponderosa Road 56-73161	Julio Montez 19 Ponderosa Road 56-71361	2.____
3.	Mary Mitchell 2314 Melbourne Drive 68-92172	Mary Mitchell 2314 Melbourne Drive 68-92172	3.____
4.	Harry Patterson 25 Dunne Street 14-33430	Harry Patterson 25 Dunne Street 14-34330	4.____
5.	Patrick Murphy 171 West Hosmer Street 93-81214	Patrick Murphy 171 West Hosmer Street 93-18214	5.____
6.	August Schultz 816 St. Clair Avenue 53-40149	August Schultz 816 St. Claire Avenue 53-40149	6.____
7.	George Taft 72 Runnymede Street 47-04033	George Taft 72 Runnymede Street 47-04023	7.____
8.	Angus Henderson 1418 Madison Street 81-76375	Angus Henderson 1318 Madison Street 81-76375	8.____

COLUMN I

9. Carolyn Mazur
   12 Riverview Road
   38-99615

10. Adele Russell
    1725 Lansing Lane
    72-91962

COLUMN II

Carolyn Mazur
12 Rivervane Road
38-99615

Adela Russell
1725 Lansing Lane
72-91962

9.____

10.____

KEY (CORRECT ANSWERS)

1.	C	6.	B
2.	C	7.	C
3.	D	8.	D
4.	C	9.	B
5.	C	10.	A

TEST 4

DIRECTIONS: Questions 1 through 20 test how good you are at catching mistakes in typing or printing. In each question, the name and address in Column II should be an exact copy of the name and address in Column I. Mark your answer
A. If there is no mistake in either name or address;
B. If there is a mistake in both name and address;
C. If there is a mistake only in the name;
D. If there is a mistake only in the address.

PRINT THE LETTER OF THE CORRECT ANSWER IN THE SPACE AT THE RIGHT.

COLUMN I	COLUMN II	
1. Milos Yanocek 33-60 14 Street Long Island City, N.Y. 11011	Milos Yanocek 33-60 14 Street Long Island City, N.Y. 11001	1.____
2. Alphonse Sabattelo 24 Minnetta Lane New York, N.Y. 10006	Alphonse Sabbattelo 24 Minetta Lane New York, N.Y. 10006	2.____
3. Helen Steam 5 Metropolitan Oval Bronx, N.Y. 10462	Helene Stearn 5 Metropolitan Oval Bronx, N.Y. 10462	3.____
4. Jacob Weisman 231 Francis Lewis Boulevard Forest Hills, N.Y. 11325	Jacob Weisman 231 Francis Lewis Boulevard Forest Hills, N.Y. 11325	4.____
5. Riccardo Fuente 134 West 83 Street New York, N.Y. 10024	Riccardo Fuentes 134 West 88 Street New York, N.Y. 10024	5.____
6. Dennis Lauber 52 Avenue D Brooklyn, N.Y. 11216	Dennis Lauder 52 Avenue D Brooklyn, N.Y. 11216	6.____
7. Paul Cutter 195 Galloway Avenue Staten Island, N.Y. 10356	Paul Cutter 175 Galloway Avenue Staten Island, N.Y. 10365	7.____
8. Sean Donnelly 45-58 41 Avenue Woodside, N.Y. 11168	Sean Donnelly 45-58 41 Avenue Woodside, N.Y. 11168	8.____
9. Clyde Willot 1483 Rockaway Avenue Brooklyn, N.Y. 11238	Clyde Willat 1483 Rockaway Avenue Brooklyn, N.Y. 11238	9.____

COLUMN I

COLUMN II

10. Michael Stanakis
419 Sheriden Avenue
Staten Island, N.Y. 10363

Michael Stanakis
419 Sheraden Avenue
Staten Island, N.Y. 10363

10.____

11. Joseph DiSilva
63-84 Saunders Road
Rego Park, N.Y. 11431

Joseph Disilva
64-83 Saunders Road
Rego Park, N.Y. 11431

11.____

12. Linda Polansky
2224 Fendon Avenue
Bronx, N.Y. 20464

Linda Polansky
2255 Fenton Avenue
Bronx, N.Y. 10464

12.____

13. Alfred Klein
260 Hillside Terrace
Staten Island, N.Y. 15545

Alfred Klein
260 Hillside Terrace
Staten Island, N.Y. 15545

13.____

14. William McDonnell
504 E. 55 Street
New York, N.Y. 10103

William McConnell
504 E. 55 Street
New York, N.Y. 10108

14.____

15. Angela Cipolla
41-11 Parson Avenue
Flushing, N.Y. 11446

Angela Cipola
41-11 Parsons Avenue
Flushing, N.Y. 11446

15.____

16. Julie Sheridan
1212 Ocean Avenue
Brooklyn, N.Y. 11237

Julia Sheridan
1212 Ocean Avenue
Brooklyn, N.Y. 11237

16.____

17. Arturo Rodriguez
2156 Cruger Avenue
Bronx, N.Y. 10446

Arturo Rodrigues
2156 Cruger Avenue
Bronx, N.Y. 10446

17.____

18. Helen McCabe
2044 East 19 Street
Brooklyn, N.Y. 11204

Helen McCabe
2040 East 19 Street
Brooklyn, N.Y. 11204

18.____

19. Charles Martin
526 West 160 Street
New York, N.Y. 10022

Charles Martin
526 West 160 Street
New York, N.Y. 10022

19.____

20. Morris Rabinowitz
31 Avenue M
Brooklyn, N.Y. 11216

Morris Rabinowitz
31 Avenue N
Brooklyn, N.Y. 11216

20.____

3 (#4)

KEY (CORRECT ANSWERS)

1. D	11. B
2. B	12. D
3. C	13. A
4. A	14. B
5. B	15. B

6. C	16. C
7. D	17. C
8. A	18. D
9. B	19. A
10. D	20. D

TEST 5

DIRECTIONS: In copying the addresses below from Column A to the same line in Column B, an Agent-in-Training made some errors. For Questions 1 through 5, if you find that the agent made an error in
only one line, mark your answer A;
only two lines, mark your answer B;
only three lines, mark your answer C;
all four lines, mark your answer D.

EXAMPLE

COLUMN A	COLUMN B
24 Third Avenue	24 Third Avenue
5 Lincoln Road	5 Lincoln Street
50 Central Park West	6 Central Park West
37-21 Queens Boulevard	21-37 Queens Boulevard

Since errors were made on only three lines, namely the second, third, and fourth, the CORRECT answer is C.
PRINT THE LETTER OF THE CORRECT ANSWER IN THE SPACE AT THE RIGHT.

	COLUMN A	COLUMN B	
1.	57-22 Springfield Boulevard 94 Gun Hill Road 8 New Dorp Lane 36 Bedford Avenue	75-22 Springfield Boulevard 94 Gun Hill Avenue 8 New Drop Lane 36 Bedford Avenue	1.____
2.	538 Castle Hill Avenue 54-15 Beach Channel Drive 21 Ralph Avenue 162 Madison Avenue	538 Castle Hill Avenue 54-15 Beach Channel Drive 21 Ralph Avenue 162 Morrison Avenue	2.____
3.	49 Thomas Street 27-21 Northern Blvd. 86 125th Street 872 Atlantic Ave.	49 Thomas Street 21-27 Northern Blvd. 86 125th Street 872 Baltic Ave,	3.____
4.	261-17 Horace Harding Expwy. 191 Fordham Road 6 Victory Blvd. 552 Oceanic Ave.	261-17 Horace Harding Pkwy. 191 Fordham Road 6 Victoria Blvd. 552 Ocean Ave.	4.____
5.	90-05 38th Avenue 19 Central Park West 9281 Avenue X 22 West Farms Square	90-05 36th Avenue 19 Central Park East 9281 Avenue X 22 West Farms Square	5.____

2 (#5)

KEY (CORRECT ANSWERS)

1. C
2. A
3. B
4. C
5. B

———

TEST 6

DIRECTIONS: For Questions 1 through 10, choose the letter in Column II next to the number which EXACTLY matches the number in Column I. *PRINT THE LETTER OF THE CORRECT ANSWER IN THE SPACE AT THE RIGHT.*

	COLUMN I	COLUMN II	
1.	14235	A. 13254 B. 12435 C. 13245 D. 14235	1._____
2.	70698	A. 90768 B. 60978 C. 70698] D. 70968	2._____
3.	11698	A. 11689 B. 11986 C. 11968 D. 11698	3._____
4.	50497	A. 50947 B. 50497 C. 50749 D. 54097	4._____
5.	69635	A. 60653 B. 69630 C. 69365 D. 69635	5._____
6.	1201022011	A. 1201022011 B. 1201020211 C. 1202012011 D. 1021202011	6._____
7.	3893981389	A. 3893891389 B. 3983981389 C. 3983891389 D. 3893981389	7._____
8.	4765476589	A. 4765476598 B. 4765476588 C. 4765476589 D. 4765746589	8._____

9. 8679678938
    A. 8679687938
    B. 8679678938
    C. 8697678938
    D. 8678678938

10. 6834836932
    A. 6834386932
    B. 6834836923
    C. 6843836932
    D. 6834836932

Questions 11-15.

DIRECTIONS: For Questions 11 through 15, determine how many of the symbols in Column Z are exactly the same as the symbol in Column Y.
If none is exactly the same, answer A;
If only one symbol is exactly the same, answer B;
If two symbols are exactly the same, answer C;
If three symbols are exactly the same, answer D.

COLUMN Y	COLUMN Z
11. A123B1266	A123B1366 A123B1266 A133B1366 A123B1266
12. CC28D3377	CD22D3377 CC38D3377 CC28C3377 CC28D2277
13. M21AB201X	M12AB201X M21AB201X M21AB201Y M21BA201X
14. PA383Y744	AP383Y744 PA338Y744 PA388Y744 PA383Y774
15. PB2Y8893	PB2Y8893 PB2Y8893 PB3Y8898 PB2Y8893

KEY (CORRECT ANSWERS)

1.	D	6.	A	11.	C
2.	C	7.	D	12.	A
3.	D	8.	C	13.	B
4.	B	9.	B	14.	A
5.	D	10.	D	15.	D